CALIFORNIA

East *of* Yosemite

A VISITOR'S GUIDE

Text and Photography by Paul Wellens

Edition ISBNs:

Softcover   978-0-9802425-2-2
Hardcover   978-0-9802425-3-9
PDF   978-0-9802425-4-6

Printed in China by Global Interprint

TOPO! is a registered trademark of National Geographic Maps

In memory of

François Wellens

1927 - 2007

My father

TABLE OF CONTENTS

LIST OF PHOTOGRAPHS

Two kinds of photographs were used to illustrate this book. The first set is small in size and used to document things like buildings, road signs etc. The list of the larger photographs in this book follows below. They are available as matted prints to decorate your home.

Contact me at paulpwellens@gmail.com or visit www.paulpwellens.com to check on available sizes and pricing

PREFACE

I discovered this area in California, located east of Yosemite National Park, more than 12 years ago. Immediately I fell in love with the region. Since that day I went back as often as I could.

During these years, I have driven to beautiful places, walked hiking trails with great views and met wonderful people.

I photographed most of the areas that I visited and studied the interesting history of the region by reading many of the excellent books that are available.

This book is all about sharing with you, the reader, my passion and enthusiasm for this wonderful part of the world.

It is also a guide to help you plan a vacation there, with information on where to visit, stay, hike, eat, etc. More important than you might think, it also explains in which time of the year to do that.

The book contains a selection of my favorite places you can drive to or hike to, illustrated with my own photographs, some interesting anecdotes and trivia, and has been ten years in the making.

There is no intent for it to contain every hike or location in the Eastern Sierra, but there is enough here to fill a two to three week vacation.

I have structured the book as a set of day trips from one central location, the town of *June Lake*. I have found this to be the ideal spot to drop off your suitcase and explore the Eastern Sierra for as many days as you have time. In Chapter Three I will describe in more detail why I feel June Lake is the place.

Subsequent chapters describe a different section, north or south on US HWY 395, with places to visit and trail heads to drive to for a wonderful hike. US HWY 395, nicknamed *El Camino Sierra*, is the main road going through the Eastern Sierra and is one of the most beautiful roads in the country.

The intent is that there should no be more than 200 miles of driving a day. After all, this should be a vacation.

At the end of the book I also include chapters on Yosemite Valley and Death Valley National Park.

This breaks the 200 mile rule, but maybe this is where you will be driving through towards your next destination. I just do not want you to miss out on my favorite spots in those National Parks.

The idea for writing a book about this area came many years ago, for another reason. In all those years. I met many people that were en route to or coming from Yosemite National Park without any time to stop and actually see something.

Most of them would have just crossed Tioga Pass coming from the park or had been driving a whole day coming from destinations further east such as Las Vegas or Death Valley. They would be seeking lodging and food. Sometimes none would be available.

Many tourists travelling east, cross Tioga Pass late in the day believing it is easy to find a place to stay, and the accommodation in Lee Vining, the first town they reach, is limited.

Those travelling west, earlier in the year, do not know that Tioga Pass is still closed. To them, Yosemite Valley is now suddenly 500 miles away.

Tioga Pass is a key element of this region. At almost 10,000 ft., it can still be closed in early July.

This is how these people discover places like Lee Vining or June Lake: as part of a voyage that could turn into a trip from hell. The purpose of this book is to avoid those surprises and make this area a planned portion of a wonderful vacation.

In the summer time, thousands of European tourists visit the area, often with an itinerary that is either given by a tour operator or based on the information found in guides published in Europe. I checked several of those guides on California, as a test. In one title, the author switched from Yosemite Valley to Mono Lake in half a page, not mentioning that it is 70 miles and that you need to cross a mountain pass that has an elevation of 9,900 ft.

In this book, I spend two chapters on just the Tioga Road alone, giving you ample opportunity to explore all the beauty around it.

I hope, dear reader, that this book, its information and its photographs, will inspire you to visit the area that I ended up loving so much. You never know, we might run into each other at the Tiger Bar or Tom's Place.

Paul Wellens

Palo Alto, February 2008

ACKNOWLEDGMENTS

This book would not have been possible without the assistance and encouragement of many people.

First and foremost I would like to express my gratitude to my parents. They are the ones that put me on this world and allowed me to study. They also planted a seed for my later love for nature and mountains by taking me to Switzerland on many summer vacations while I was a child. And the same mom and dad permitted me to leave Belgium and go seek my fortune in the United States, now more than 20 years ago.

My parents and I were fortunate to spend a week together in June Lake in the year 2001. That way they were able to experience the beauty of the place their son loves so much first hand.

Next I would like to thank all my friends who all helped me with the book by offering their expertise.

I would like to thank my friend James *"book man"* Harris for the many hours spent discussing literary topics and book publishing themes.

I thank Michael Stevenson, graphic designer, who tried to convince me not to do everything myself: photography and text and layout etc. He did not talk me out of it but thanks to his help I learned how to think like a graphic designer when it was needed. Many of his suggestions are incorporated into the book.

My gratitude also goes to Bob Alden who offered his ear on so many occasions allowing me to brainstorm about my book. Thanks to all the others who helped me with editing, in particular Pennie Custer at the Mammoth Lakes Welcome Center.

I also appreciate all the folks at the local brewery restaurant in Palo Alto for their interest, encouragement and support of my photography, and the opportunity to display my artwork. It is the photography that ultimately led to the book.

And last but not least there are all the nice folks of June lake. Without their encouragement, this project would have never seen its completion.

Thanks to Candy, John, Jeremy, Jeff, Cherie, Dale, Lesley, Jake, Terry, Shannon, Cindy, Tiffany, Rick, Prince, the resident cat who always greets me the moment I arrive, the late Wayne Wilson, a great cook and storyteller, and many, many more.

Without those wonderful people, June Lake would not be the town it is today.

CALIFORNIA

East *of* Yosemite

A VISITOR'S GUIDE

THE SIERRA NEVADA

The Sierra Nevada is the longest, highest and most spectacular mountain range in the lower 48 states of the U.S. It is situated almost entirely in California and consists of many peaks that are approaching 15,000 ft. in altitude, with Mt. Whitney as the highest.

The Sierra Nevada is a very interesting formation from a geological point of view. What will become apparent on your travels is that the western slope is a gradual, up to 80 mile long incline, with a much shorter, steeper decline on the eastern side. The region east of the Sierra Nevada mountain range is fittingly called the Eastern Sierra.

Indian people have lived there for as long as 8,000 years. When the first white men visited the area, they found primarily Miwoks where Yosemite is today and Mono Paiutes on the east side.

In the beginning of the 19th century white men tried to cross the mountain range. Jedediah S. Smith was probably the first one to achieve that crossing in the west-east direction in 1827. He travelled over the crest near what is Ebbets Pass today. Lieutenant Joseph Redderford Walker was part of a party that managed the first east-west crossing, in 1833. Based on the descriptions in their travel log they must have been the first white men to have seen Yosemite Valley, even though they never visited it.

They were also the first visitors of the Big Trees. A year later, Walker crossed the Sierra in the other direction using a route further south, after finding a pass that now bares his name. After the Gold Rush in 1849, many people came from all parts of the country and tried to cross the Sierra, looking for mining opportunities. This is when they started settling in the area, not without conflicts with the Indians living there.

The Owens Valley - a century later

Once you reach the eastern side of the Sierra Nevada the landscape appears a lot drier than on the western side It is almost desert like and is the beginning of a region called the Great Basin. The Great Basin stretches all the way into Nevada and further east to Utah. But you will notice another high mountain range not too far east, these are the White Mountains.

In between those two mountain ranges is the **Owens Valley**, which is remarkably undeveloped. This could be considered a blessing in disguise if there ever was one. About a century ago, the Department of Water and Power of Los

Mount Whitney and the Alabama Hills as seen from Lone Pine

Angeles started building an aqueduct, intercepting the water flowing down from the Sierras when the snow melts in late spring, basically converting the Owens River into a river made of concrete: the aqueduct!.

That is why what 100 years ago were green pastures, grazing cattle, peach orchards, vineyards even, has become the dry land the Owens Valley is today. Of course, it could have also turned into another overdeveloped area.

With the exception of the towns of Mammoth Lakes and Bishop there is almost no development between Bridgeport and Lone Pine, which is the area this book is covering.

Thanks to excellent roads and good accommodations we all have access to the region, its beauty, its mountains and lakes and its tranquility. I sincerely hope it will be maintained as the paradise it is today for many years to come and for many generations to cherish.

In the pages that follow, I am guiding you through the Eastern Sierra, its towns, its lakes, some of its most interesting hiking trails and its people and history. Welcome to the **wild side of California.**

Above: June lake, one of many lakes in the Eastern Sierra you can drive or hike to
Opposite: The Eastern Sierra has great fall colors in a lot of its canyons

PLANNING YOUR TRIP - ITINERARY

Now that you know where you are going, it is time to learn how to get there. As adventurous it may sound to visit a seemingly remote area of California, it is not recommended to just go there without any planning.

Do not drive to where you can get that day and then look for a place to stay. There are times of the year you cannot simply get there, because the roads are closed. Other times everybody else appears to be there as well and no rooms are available.

The busiest times of the year are the peak of the summer season, in Yosemite, and the fly fishing season in the Eastern Sierra. You can see fishermen from the first weekend in May until late fall. Traffic is, of course, always busy on weekends. This is why, on my journeys, I try to return on a Monday, a day after the other million drivers.

Memorial Day, 4th of July and Labor Day are by far the busiest weekends, just like almost everywhere else.

Memorial Day even has a different name in the Eastern Sierra. It is called **Mule Day**! In the town of Bishop the largest non-motorized parade in the country, takes place that weekend.

It comes with mules of course, they have rodeos etc. No hotel rooms are available 100 miles in either direction, unless you have made a reservation. So the message here is loud and clear: book in advance!

There are many motels in the area, campgrounds as well. This makes Visitor Centers very important. There you find up to date information on weather, road conditions and lodging, so you can plan your next destination.

But for the very first stop of the trip making a reservation way ahead of time is the right way to go.

All the destinations in this guide can be reached by car, no high clearance vehicle or 4x4 is required. Keep in mind however that there is not a gas station on every corner. So fill up the tank before you start your day trip or when it is time to leave for the next major destination. There can be 100 miles of road without a gas station, but that usually means no traffic as well.

Once you have completed the planning stage you need to determine what to take along on your trip. Not all items may be available in the Eastern Sierra and you do not want to spend your valuable vacation time shopping if you can do this beforehand.

Opposite: Aspen trees along Silver Lake - June Lake Loop

Planning Tips

Chains

The California vehicle code mandates to put chains on your tires when the weather conditions call for it. In the Eastern Sierra this can happen any day of the year. Caltrans stations will help you with that. I bought tire chains for my car hoping I will never have to use them. So far, so good. Carry chains in the trunk and make sure they match the size of your tires.

Maps

Let me tell you a story. I ran into some people in June Lake that I know. They were looking at a map, so I asked: "Where do you plan to go to today?" They said: "Probably Kings Canyon". "I don't think so" I said.

This is a 400 mile drive from June Lake. Why did they think they could drive there in half a day? On a map, the distance between Lone Pine and Kings Canyon is less than an inch.

However, what could appear as a short drive has a major obstacle: Mt. Whitney, the highest mountain. There is no road there..

Looking at a map can be deceiving! Another good example is the 1/4 inch red stripe near Tioga Pass that reads: *closed in winter* on almost every map of California. It does not tell you that winter can end as late as July and that the red stripe represents 46 miles of road!

So get some good road maps. If you are a AAA member, and you should be, go to a AAA office, and get some of their excellent free maps. Members of similar organizations from other countries, like ADAC and VTB, can enjoy the same service.

Interstates, US Highways and State Routes

In these chapters I describe many roads to guide you to various destinations. Of course you will also look for them on these maps. All main roads in California have a number. They distinguish between Interstates (blue road signs) US Highways (white signs) and State Routes (green signs).

Good examples are Interstate 5, I-5 in short, US Highway 395, US 395 in short, which is the main artery going through the Eastern Sierra and State Route 158, SR 158 in short, the June Lake Loop. Throughout this book we

will use the short description as in the above example. For a detailed description on all California numbered highways, visit *http://www.cahighways.org*

Topo Maps

If you are serious about hiking you want topographic maps as well, showing the terrain and the trails. Most Visitor Centers sell them so for these items you can wait until you are already there and give these wonderful places some business.

Recently, a new set of maps were published, called **Sierra Maps**. They have a very good one on June Lake and can be found in the local stores in June Lake and Mammoth.

Good gear

At a minimum, you want to bring a pair of good hiking boots, possibly hiking poles. I found the poles to increase my hiking capacity. Bring some warm clothing, even in the summertime. Some days it can be cold at night or even during the day at high elevations when there is a sudden change of weather.

One item I have that makes hiking a lot easier is a Camelback. This is a backpack that also has a container inside to store water and a tube to suck on to drink. Carrying water, a lot of it, is very important on hikes, in particular at high elevations. Buy the three liter model.

Photography tips

This whole region is a photographer's paradise. If you like taking pictures, and you should, I recommend a light-weight tripod, carbon fiber or basalt, that you can fit in the backpack, and some small fixed focal lenses. This is a lot less heavy than a big fat zoom lens.

To take landscape pictures, use a high f-stop and long shutter speed to maximize depth of field. That is why it is best to use a tripod. If you have a macro lens, bring it along too as these are perfect for shooting wildflowers, which are abundant in the summer time. And then there are deer, marmots, and other mammals that will not wait until you set up your tripod. For these shots you want shallow depth of field instead.

Now that the trip is planned, you have your maps and gear, packed the suitcase and loaded the car, it is time to actually get to our destination.

As mentioned in the Preface we are headed towards June Lake. Even if you stay elsewhere, such as in Lee Vining, Bishop or Mammoth Lakes, the directions below are very valid as these towns are all located along US 395 and very few miles apart.

Most, if not all, visitors will be travelling from the San Francisco Bay Area, Los Angeles or Las Vegas. Las Vegas directions are covered in Chapter 14, *Death Valley National Park.*

Directions From the San Francisco Bay Area

I live in Palo Alto, in the San Francisco Bay Area. The distance to June Lake from there is about 250 miles. I recommend leaving early enough to avoid commuter traffic in the East Bay and get across the mountains before it is dark. Estimate 6-7 hours for the journey. There are several roads crossing the Sierra Nevada to choose from.

Your beautiful, relaxing drive will take you through a constantly changing landscape. Once the East Bay is behind you, the drive takes you through the *Central Valley*, where all the California fruit is grown. Stop at a fruit stand and buy some local produce.

Next you enter the Sierra Foothills, cross SR 49, the heart of the Gold Country and then make your ascent of the Sierra. You are gradually entering a world where the elevation, in feet, listed on the green signs along the road, outnumbers the population.! This, to me, always means I am one mile closer to paradise.

Tioga Road, through Yosemite National Park.

The route I recommend is different from what you will find in other guides. The key difference is to take SR 132.

From the South Bay go over either the Dumbarton or San Mateo Bridge, take I-880 North and then I-580 East. From San Francisco, cross the Bay Bridge, take I-880 South and I-580 East. Stay on I-580 when I-580 forks to the right, direction Los Angeles. After a few miles there is a junction with SR 132 to your right.

Take SR 132. The road will swing to the left and cross I-580 and several miles later also cross I-5. After about 40 miles it will take you into the town of *Modesto*. Carefully follow the signs to stay on SR 132. Fill the tank.

Along Tioga Road in early season

You reach SR 49 in the Gold Country town of **Coulterville**. Cross SR 49 and take Main Street. This turns into a slightly winding road and, after 14 miles, joins SR 120, about 20 miles before Yosemite National Park.

Once you reach the Park you are only 75 miles from June Lake. Note that Yosemite Valley, covered in Chapter 13, is still 25 miles away. Pay the

Jeffery Hotel - Coulterville

entrance fee. It is $20 per vehicle, $25 starting in 2008, and valid for 7 days. If you have more Parks in your future within the next 12 months, purchase a **National Parks and Federal Recreational Lands pass** ($80).

About 12 miles into the Park is the turn-off for the Tioga Road. The Crane Flat Chevron Station is there as well. There are no more gas stations for another 56 miles. This road leads to Tioga Pass, the East entrance of the Park, over 9900 feet in elevation and the one part of Yosemite that has surprised many visitors by ... being closed!

You can always check Caltrans using your phone (recommended) by calling 1-800-427-7623 and typing in the road number (120) for up to date road conditions: or visit **http://www.dot. ca.gov/cgi-bin/roads.cgi**.

Assuming all is well turn left at the Tioga Road junction and enter paradise, hopefully without too much traffic. Be courteous to other drivers and respect the 45 mile traffic limit by driving not too fast but also not too slow! After all, to some this is just a highway.

If you want to enjoy the view, park on the side of the road where it is allowed, and use the turnouts to let others pass.

You reach Tioga Pass after 46 miles. Then the road descents into the Mono Basin, dropping 3000 ft. in 6 miles. Other than that this road is relatively fast. Do not get carried away and keep it under 50 mph! 12 miles after the pass you reach the junction of US 395.

Notice the Mobil station right before it. It is a gourmet restaurant in disguise. The locals go there for dinner; ever had lobster taquitos?

Turn right on US 395, drive for about 10 miles, until you reach the South June Lake junction. If needed, fill the tank at the Shell station on the corner, as there is no gas station in June Lake. Turn right at the junction, pass the first lake, June, and enter town. You can congratulate yourself: once again you have entered paradise, for the second time in a single day!

A different option

A faster, but busier, route through Yosemite is to take SR 120 from beginning to end. Follow the same directions as in the previous section, I-580 East, SR 132 East, but when SR 132 is about to cross I-5, take I-5 north for about 10 miles until you enter Lathrop. Take the SR 120 exit. You are now on the combined SR 108 and 120. Ten miles before the town of Sonora you need to take a right turn to follow SR 120 into Yosemite, through the Gold Country town of **Groveland**.

Sonora Pass

If you want to avoid the Yosemite weekend traffic, and take a different road, a very good option is to go over **Sonora Pass**. The drive is a little longer, as it puts you on US 395 about 50 miles north of June Lake but those miles are very fast ones. The total distance to June Lake is about 280 miles.

Sonora Pass, on SR 108, usually opens weeks before Tioga Pass does. The portion of SR 120 that lies inside the Park is managed by the National Park Service. That stretch of the Tioga road is subject to avalanches once the snow starts to melt, which can delay opening day. Once the Park opens it is expected to remain open. Caltrans has more flexibility to close and reopen Sonora Pass early in the season.

One year, I took Sonora Pass on the very day it opened. It was beautiful. I felt like my car was the only one on the road for about 100 miles!

Follow the same directions listed in the previous section to get to SR 120: I-580 East, SR 132 East, I-5 north, SR 120 East. Do not take a right turn ten miles before Sonora, but keep going. The road bypasses the actual center of town. If you do have extra time, make a detour to check out the town itself, to get a flavor of the Gold Country, or visit nearby Columbia State Park. This is an open air museum, all about the Gold Rush. It also has one of the oldest Wells Fargo bank buildings.

Fill the tank in Sonora or one of the small towns just east of it (e.g. Miwok Village) as there are no gas stations for another 80 miles.

SR 108 is a relatively fast road, often more than two lanes until about seven miles before the summit, at **Kennedy Meadows**. There the road narrows and has a lot of sharp curves until the summit. Sonora Pass itself has an elevation of 9624 ft., only 300 ft. lower than Tioga Pass. Once you cross the summit it goes downhill real fast, so make sure your brakes are all right.

Along Sonora Pass opening day

Wells Fargo Bank Building

Near Leavitt Meadows, on the east side of the pass, is a hairpin turn with a safe spot to stop, giving you a great view at a canyon through which the Walker river flows.

A few miles before US 395 you pass a military camp where many U.S. soldiers were trained to prepare for Operation Desert Storm, because of the similarities of the terrain. On your way down you may even see signs stating **Warning: military crossing**.

When you reach US 395, turn right and drive south, through the town of Bridgeport, pass the turnoff to Bodie, make a stop at the Mono Lake Vista Point at Conway Summit, and drive through the town of Lee Vining, while admiring more of Mono Lake.

Notice the Visitor Center on the left just before town, as well as the big blue sign in the middle of town **Visitor Information**. That is the home of the Mono Lake Committee, mentioned in Chapter Four.

Drive another ten miles to the South June Lake Junction. Fill the tank at the Shell station on the corner, if needed. There are no gas stations in the town of June Lake.

Turn right at the junction, pass the first lake, June, and enter town. Welcome to paradise!

SR 4 and Ebbets Pass

This is, in my opinion, the most beautiful of all roads going across the Sierra Nevada. It is also happens to be the oldest one. It is more driving, a little over 300 miles, but most of it is actually very fast. Along the way, there are a lot of interesting places to visit.

That is why I recommend spending a night halfway in places like Murphys before continuing on. See Chapter 12 on SR 4 and Ebbets Pass for details.

Alternate Roads

If the roads mentioned so far are closed, there are still a few alternatives.

Except on a day of actual snowfall, SR 88 is open year-round. From the Bay Area, take I-580 East to I-132 East, then I-5 north to Stockton. Do not get on SR 4 but keep going north for a mile or two and take SR 88 East to the town of Jackson in the Gold Country. From there follow SR 88 through the ski resort of **Kirkwood**.

Once you cross **Carson Pass** you will reach a junction with State Route SR 89, close to Lake Tahoe.

SR 88 equals SR 89 for a while until the junction to Markleeville and **Monitor Pass**. I assume you have chosen this route as because Monitor Pass is closed, so continue on SR 88 into Nevada. You will enter the twin towns of Minden and Gardnerville on US 395, just south of Carson City. Turn right once you reach US 395.

A true last resort would be to cross the Bay Bridge in San Francisco, take I-80, and catch US 395 in Reno. This is still a better option than taking I-5 south to Bakersfield, driving east to HWY 395 near Ridgecrest and then driving 200 miles north on US 395 from there: a 400 mile detour - not necessary.

Directions from the Los Angeles Basin

I lived in Venice Beach, CA, close to Santa Monica. I hope that many visitors of this wonderful state will include the Los Angeles beaches in their itinerary. My first visit to Santa Monica resulted in a turning point in my life: I moved to California.

Directions start in Santa Monica. The distance to June Lake is about 335 miles. Plan for seven hours of driving. The first 50 miles are the ones subject to traffic conditions, the rest is smooth sailing.

Take I-10, the Santa Monica Freeway, East to I-405 North, the San Diego Freeway. Go over Sepulveda Pass and cross US 101. Eventually, I-405 joins I-5 north. Follow it, then exit on SR 14, the Antelope Valley Freeway.

This will take you through Santa Clarita, Palmdale and Lancaster and eventually **Mojave**. You have now driven 90 miles, hopefully without too much traffic. I suggest you fill the tank here. The next gas station is at least 50 miles away. Turn right on the traffic light where SR 14 continues.

You have entered the Mojave desert. There is no reason to panic, on the contrary, deserts are beautiful. Notice all the Joshua trees. This area is also the southern tip of the Sierra Nevada mountain range. As you drive north, the peaks on your left are getting increasingly higher. 110 miles later, in **Lone Pine**, you will see the highest one, **Mt. Whitney**.

About 45 miles north of Mojave, SR 14 ends and joins US 395. Keep going north. Notice the billboards advertising places that are still 80 miles away. The first time I saw that I thought it was very funny to see a billboard "**Taco Bell 80 miles**" in the middle of the desert. US 395 will take you through Lone Pine, Independence, Big Pine, Bishop, along Mammoth Lakes and then reach the June Lake Junction after driving 335 miles from the beach. Beach and mountains in one day. This is California !

There are some interesting places along the way to June Lake. If you have no plans to return here as part of a day trip you should make a few stops. They are described in chapter ten, **Bishop to Lone Pine**.

The obvious one is the Visitor Center in Lone Pine. Better still, you could consider spending one night in Lone Pine to cut the driving in half. That would allow you to have great views of **Owens Lake** in the afternoon, and drive to the **Alabama Hills** the next morning. You can visit the Movie Museum in Lone Pine and many more places on the way to June Lake.

Joshua tree in the Mojave Desert

III

JUNE LAKE

The **June Lake Loop** is a 15 mile road that loops around 4 lakes and a ski area, June Mountain. It begins and ends on US highway 395. The southern junction has a gas station and a gift shop. One mile west is another junction with a road to the ski area that bypasses the actual town of June Lake.

This spot is called the **Oh! Ridge** for obvious reasons. There is a small parking lot with a vista tower and most visitors will have their first ever view of the lake June Lake from this location. The view itself is dominated by Carson Peak.

After about another mile, as you pass a huge boulder (705 tons) you enter the town of **June Lake**. Notice the sign: Pop. 613, elevation 7600 ft. The road then curves around **Gull Lake**, goes by the ski area and next through

Opposite : June Lake in the fall

the other half of town. After a sharp S curve in the road by the power plant you will drive alongside **Silver Lake**.

Here begins the northern half of the loop, which is closed in the winter time. It is very spectacular in the fall when the leaves of all the aspen trees turn yellow and gold.

On the other side of the lake you pass the Silver Lake Resort and the pack station. The loop continues along Rush Creek, goes slightly uphill by Grant Lake, a reservoir, and then follows a straight line back down to US 395.

When to go ?

Although the town of June Lake is accessible all year long I recommend going between the end of May and the middle of October. The fishing season usually starts on the first of May. The

last time I was there on Opening Day the lake (June) was still frozen for the most part, but it did not stop the fishing contest from taking place.

From July to September of course it is summer in the Sierra. The snow has started to melt, the temperatures are very nice, the hiking trails are open and, more importantly, so are all the passes across the Sierra Nevada.

History

Rumor has it that the town of June Lake has its name because you had to wait until June before it can actually be reached. As is the case with the entire region of the Eastern Sierra the inhabitants were Paiute Indians. The first white men probably laid eyes on what is now June Lake around 1870. Even these first visitors probably came there for one reason: to fish!

Very early on the region was known for its good fishing. It took a while to get there, as there were no roads. US 395 did not exist yet, nor did the June Lake Loop. The canyon was known as **Horseshoe Canyon**. If you follow the loop, you can tell why, as the canyon is shaped like a horseshoe.

In the early days the lakes had different names. What is now June Lake was called Summit, Gull Lake was Granite Lake, Silver Lake was Goose Lake, and of course Grant Lake did not exist yet. One reference I could find of the current names of the lakes dates back to 1929, but others suggest the current names were established earlier.

One of those fishermen who came to June Lake and never went back was Roy Carson from Pasadena. He made the trip in 1916 and found a job at the then recently constructed Power Plant by Rush Creek. This facility secured electricity for the greater part of Southern California and parts of Nevada for a long time. He started building cabins by Silver Lake and this is what became Carson Camp, now known as the Silver Lake Resort. The present main building, a great place for breakfast,

Carson Peak reflecting in Silver Lake

was established in 1921. Carson Peak, 10,909 ft., is also named after him and his wife Nancy.

In 1924 the U.S. .Forest Service built a dirt road to what is now the town of June Lake and the development of the town began. June Lake became known as the *Lake of Big Fish*

On May 1, 1928, the June Lodge, the Heidelberg Inn today, was officially opened. Many movie stars would end up visiting this place. In the meantime, Los Angeles had already built an aqueduct to use the water of the Owens river as the main water supply for that city.

The town of June Lake, Gull Lake on the left, June Lake on the right.

As L. A. had grown from a 200,000 people city to one of millions the existing water supply was no longer going to be sufficient. L. A. decided to expand the aqueduct and purchased water rights in the Mono Basin. That caused June Lake to boom as workers needed a place to stay, eat and have some entertainment while they were working on the expansion of the aqueduct.

As early as 1932, the *Tiger Bar* was opened by Glen Colton. Supposedly the name came later. I was always told that at some point it was named

Tiger Bar because the nickname of the owner's son was *Tiger*.

Sometime in 1940 a Mr. Bud Kline put up a long bar with a dance floor and years later the bar and cafe buildings were moved down the canyon and became the Carson Peak Inn. If you look closely at one of the signs at that restaurant, you will notice it was painted over a sign that says: *"Bud's bar"*.

In the same year the Grant Lake dam was completed and filled by the Los Angeles Department of Water and

Power (LADWP). Also in that year the June Lake Winter Sports Association was founded and the first ski lift opened on June Mountain. A day pass was $1.

In 1941 the LADWP started diversions from Rush Creek and Lee Vining Creek into the new section of the L. A. aqueduct, resulting in the end of that project. As a result, June Lake turned into a small town again and, in a way, it still is.

Gull Lake always has aspens glowing in the fall

Visiting June Lake

The obvious places to visit in June Lake are where you already are: the town, the lakes and the loop. If you are staying in town you can stroll down the streets and walk to the June Lake and Gull Lake marinas and rent a boat there. And of course, if you are into fishing, you probably do not want to go anywhere else for a while.

If you forgot your fishing gear, you can find what you need at Ernie's fish and tackle shop - tell John or Jeremy I said Hi!. In the winter, the tackle shop transforms into a ski shop.

The east side of June Lake, which has a beach, is a great place to relax in the summertime. The shallow water is warm enough to make your feet wet or even swim. Or you can just lie down, breath the clean mountain air and get a sun tan at 7,600 ft.

There are several nice and easy walks in June lake. You can walk around Gull Lake, starting at the playground near the Marina. To complete your easy stroll, you will have to walk on the main road for a stretch.

The other easy walk, especially enjoyable in the fall, is on the other side of the loop. Between Silver Lake and Grant Lake there is a parking lot with rest rooms on the south side of the road. From there you can walk down to Rush Creek, where you will find a trail that takes you almost back to Silver. It has a few nice benches to picnic; you will run into fishermen and, occasionally, a deer!

Because of the shape of the canyon every hiking trail will immediately start with a steep incline. However, if you are in great shape and into hiking, you can get to formidable places in just a few hours, such as Fern Lake, Gem Lake, Agnew Lake and even Thousand Island Lake.

June Lake on April 30th 2005, a day before the fishing season started.

There is one moderate hike in June Lake. The trail head is across the street from the Fire Station next to the big 705 ton boulder, in the beginning of town. Its gradual ascent opens up views of the town itself first, with June and Gull. After a few switchbacks you can see Mono Lake and beyond. Hike as far as you want. The trail passes the ski area and goes to Yost Lake. That is a 4.5 mile trip one-way.

Food and Lodging

One of the nice things about June Lake is that it is not only a beautiful place and a small town, it also has a lot to offer where it comes to lodging and dining, even if dining means breakfast.

The section of town between June Lake and Gull Lake is where most of the businesses are located. I always stay in the June Lake Motel. I am that kind of person. Once I find a place I like, I go back there, and do not look for anything else.

If you stay at the June Lake Motel, please give my regards to Cherie and Dale. The place has nice rooms with a kitchen for around $100 a night. Next door is the June Lake General Store where you can buy all the necessary

Beautiful fall colors along the loop between Silver and Grant lakes

So where to go for dinner or have a beer before going to bed? My favorite place for dinner is the Carson Peak Inn, which is a 1.9 mile drive from the center of town. It is open year round from 5 p.m. until closing. Closing time for a kitchen in the Eastern Sierra could mean as early as 9 p.m.

The Carson Peak Inn offers great food at great value! All dinners include soup, salad, baked potato and whatever entree you ordered for around

Signs in front of the Carson Peak Inn

things you may have forgotten to take along on your trip. There are many other places to stay in this part of town and further along the loop.

A very unique place, even if it is just to visit for a few moments, is the Heidelberg Inn. This motel had the largest fireplace in the country in the middle of its lobby - the record was lost, the fireplace is still there - and was frequented by movie stars in the 1930's.

Check out the lobby and its photographs of Bing Crosby, Charlie Chaplin, Bustor Keaton, Bob Hope, Doro-thy Lamour etc. Frank Capra, movie director of many movies such as ***"It's a wonderful life"*** actually had a cabin near Silver Lake. A few years ago, I met the Capras (Jr.) at the Sierra Inn and saw Frank Capra the IIIrd at the Carson Peak Inn. It is a small world, and a wonderful life indeed.

Not only did movie stars vacation here, some movies were actually filmed in June Lake or/and at the Heidelberg, such as ***Road to Utopia*** with Bob Hope and Bing Crosby. In the movie they want you to believe it is set in Alaska.

ECV
E Clampus Vitus

There are many places in the Eastern Sierra, inside restaurants or at historic sites, where you can find the signs *ECV* or *E Clampus Vitus*. It is the name of an organization that I mention from time to time in this book. Members call themselves Clampers and their meeting places, usually local saloons, are referred to as Official Watering Holes. The name ECV is in Dog Latin, it reads and sounds like Latin but really has no meaning.

It is said that the organization was created in 1845 in Lewisport, Virginia. Soon there were Chapters in California, in particular in the Mother Lode due to the Gold Rush. During that time there were several organizations, new and existing, such as the Masons and the Independent Order of Odd Fellows. The name of the latter (I.O.O.F.) marks many a building in the Gold Country. Many miners were very far from home and could use an organization to hang on to and know of a place where members would help each other.

The ECV members at that time felt a less exclusive organization was needed and opened membership to most any man who had come of age. In reaction to the upscale fraternities, Clampers began dressing in red long johns and pinning on badges made of cut-out tin lids. This practice, "wearing your tin" continues to this day, with real badges, a red miner's shirt, black hat and Levi's jeans. At least once a year every Chapter holds an ECV meeting. On that day or weekend you will notice many men in red shirts in the immediate vicinity of (or inside) an Official Watering Hole. In June Lake, where all Clampers are part of Bodie Chapter 64, that would be the second weekend of September. Mark Twain was a Clamper, and it was at an ECV meeting that he heard the story which he wrote as "*The Celebrated Jumping Frog of Calaveras County*".

Today, the ECV organization remains dedicated to the preservation of the history of California. This endeavor may take the form of written works, construction and dedications of monuments, ceremonies and other special events. As recent as September 8, 2007, a monument was dedicated in June Lake, at an old mining site.

June Lake from the ridge showing Mono Lake in the background.

*Carson Peak sign, tilted. Notice **BUD'S**. Opposite: Silver Lake with boats*

$20. On busy weekends they serve Prime Rib: to die for ! Say hi to Rick for me. If you happen to sit at table one, look at my Carson Peak picture on display.

Closer to downtown June Lake is the Sierra Inn. On Saturdays they have a buffet - a great bargain!. The place is very popular for take out pizza. Folks that stay in campgrounds or nearby motels prefer this over having dinner inside a restaurant.

A very popular place is the Tiger Bar. Supposedly it is the third bar in the state of California to have obtained a liquor license after Prohibition (est. 1932) There you can go for breakfast, lunch or dinner or just have a couple of beers and hang out with the locals, play some pool and put some songs on the jukebox. It is my favorite place for breakfast. I have many of their T-shirts and hats and it's amazing in how

many places in California, or Belgium even, people recognized the logo and reacted: "The Tiger Bar! I have been there". So pay the Tiger Bar a visit and tell Jake, Terry or Shannon I said hi.

Enjoy your stay in June Lake. In the following chapters I will take you to more wonderful places to drive to, or hike to. They are all close to June Lake and the perfect ingredients for a great day trip.

MONO LAKE

As is the case with almost the entire Owens Valley, **Mono Lake** looks the way it does today due to the need for water in Los Angeles.

Mono is a Paiute Indian word that means: beautiful. I could not agree more with that description.

There are two places where you find useful information on Mono Lake: the **Mono Lake Committee** in Lee Vining and the Visitor Center just north of town. At the latter there is a permanent photo exhibit with a Mono Lake photograph on display, taken by Ansel Adams in 1948. All it shows is one big, almost boring lake.

Mono Lake looks completely different today. All the crystalline structures that have developed at the bottom of the lake, called **tufas**, are now showing up at the lake's surface and shore. When the Los Angeles Department of Water and Power started diverting water from the inlets of Mono Lake, mainly Rush Creek and Lee Vining Creek, in 1941, the lake level dropped over 40 feet in 40 years, from 6,417 to 6,372 ft. The tufa towers in and around the lake make it a unique landscape and a photographer's delight.

When to visit ?

Mono Lake is accessible all year round but the road to the most popular end of the lake, 120 East, is closed parts of winter. From June Lake, drive to the June Lake junction and then north on US 395 until 1/4 of a mile before the north end of the loop. Turn right on 120 East, marked **Benton** and drive 5 miles. Turn left at the nicely graded dirt road to the South Tufa area. A paved trail will take you to the lake's shore. An entrance fee is required at the beginning of the trail, unless you have the new **National Parks and Federal Recreational Lands pass**.

At the shore there is a trail leading you through a large collection of tufa towers. The paved trail itself has displays of some of the birds and the brushes you see, but also shows, in various spots, a sign indicating where the lake level used to be in particular years.

Where the paved trail turns into a wooden one is the targeted new lake level as a result of the recent laws that the Mono Lake Committee helped pushing through: 6,392 feet. It will be many more years before the water reaches that point.

Opposite: Tufas along the South Tufa trail. I appreciated the little clouds that came by to enhance the picture

Lee Vining Creek along the trail by the same name

History

Most of the history of Mono Lake is its natural and geological history. At 500,000 years it is one of the oldest lakes in North America. Many good books are available on the natural history of the Sierra Nevada and the Great Basin.

The Mono Lake Committee bookstore in Lee Vining has an excellent selection. They also publish a few thin field guides. I recommend you purchase some.

As mentioned before, it was 1941 when the LADWP started diverting water from the inlets to Mono Lake. Notice that the lake has no outlets, so where does the water go? It evaporates. Consequently it is now about 2.5 times as saline as the Pacific Ocean. The water is also very alkaline. Its pH is about 10, just like soap.

None other than **Mark Twain** has a great description of Mono Lake in his adorable book "**Roughing it**". One of my favorite quotes is the following:

"Its sluggish waters are so strong with alkali that if you only dip the most hopelessly soiled garment into them once or twice, and wring it out, it will be found as clean as if it had been through the ablest of washer-women's hands."

In 1978, the Mono Lake Committee was formed by the late **David Gaines** to drive an effort to protect Mono Lake and its natural habitats. As a result of the lobbying efforts of the Mono Lake Committee and others, the Mono Lake

Tufa State Reserve was created in 1981, and the Mono Basin National Forest Scenic Area in 1984.

In 1994 the State Water Resources Control Board issued Decision 1631, which set minimum flows for the streams, set limits on water exports based on the level of Mono Lake, designed to raise and stabilize the lake at a level 20 feet above its lowest level, and ordered LADWP to restore the streams and waterfowl habitat.

The lake elevation afforded by the decision, 6,392 feet is still 25 feet below Mono Lake's pre-diversion level of 6,417 feet, but it will at least salvage and restore most of it natural habitat and unique ecosystem.

Visit **http://www.monolake.org** for more details and up to date information on the excellent work by the Mono Lake Committee, or better still, become a member.

The Mono Lake Ecosystem

Mono Lake has an interesting ecosystem. There are no fish in the lake, but millions of tiny little brine shrimp and countless alkaline flies, the most human friendly flies I have

Mono Lake Committee headquarters. It has an excellent selection of books

Storm over Mono Lake

ever seen. Once you reach the shore they will kindly fly out of your way. Both shrimp and flies feed of the algae in the lake and are in turn the food source to all the various species of birds that populate the lake.

There are two islands in the lake where thousands of seagulls nest until it is time to move on again. You may have wondered why there are seagulls 250 miles from the nearest ocean. Should the lake level sink any deeper, predators such as coyotes could actually reach these islands and destroy the ecosystem.

What are tufas ?

The word tufa is Latin and is the name for an unusual geological form of calcite rock. The Romans used it for many buildings and bridges. Tufa is essentially common limestone. What is uncommon about this limestone is the way it forms.

Typically, underwater springs coming from the mountains when the snow melts, rich in calcium, mix with lake water rich in carbonates. A chemical reaction occurs resulting in calcium carbonate: limestone. The calcium carbonate solidifies around the spring,

ono Craters. The Mono Basin and Mammoth area is volcanic terrain

and a tufa tower will grow. Tufa towers grow exclusively underwater, and some grow to heights of over 30 feet. Once above water they become extremely fragile, so do not climb on them and don't take samples with you.

More fun at Mono Lake

Check at the visitor kiosk if there is a guided tour the day you are visiting. The Mono Lake Committee people do a great job explaining the whole Mono Lake ecosystem. It is especially recommended when you are visiting with young children. They will even show you how to make a tufa in a bottle!

There are other parts of the lake that you can access. Near South Tufa is Navy Beach. You need to turn right on the dirt road to reach Navy Beach. I went for a swim there once and I found

Mono Lake

Mono Lake Sunrise

Mark Twain proven right about the effect of the lake on what I was wearing. I did not float though, I had to swim.

In Lee Vining there are several additional lake accesses. One spot is the old Marina, not more than a parking lot really, and then north of town you have the County Park. This is where my parents and I saw our first tufa in 1995.

Chapter Nine takes you to **Conway Summit**, which has a spectacular view overlooking the entire Mono Basin.

This is how this adventure started for me, noticing all these mountains from Conway Summit, as the photograph on the previous page shows.

Another good look at the lake is from the Visitor Center outside of town. It has a small nature trail with educational displays and you can also walk all the way back to the other side of town along the Lee Vining Creek Trail. It is fabulous in the fall.

To reach the trail head in Lee Vining, park along the road near the beginning (south side) of town. Across from the main building of the Lakeview Lodge there is a downhill walkway that takes you to the trail head. The trail follows Lee Vining Creek for a little over a mile and switches back to the Visitor Center.

Food and Lodging

I assume you are returning to June Lake. If not, there are several motels in Lee Vining, all along US 395. If you worked up an appetite, there are a few interesting places to eat I would like to recommend.

North of town is the Mono Inn, open for dinner only, owned by: **Sarah Adams**. Sarah is the granddaughter of Ansel Adams, the great photographer. The Mono Inn also contains a small gallery with Ansel Adams photographs.

If you are looking for something more casual, there is **Bodie Mike's**, next door to the Mono Lake Committee. The restaurant is open mid June to mid September. You can sit outside, watch the lake and enjoy a great burger or BBQ chicken.

Opposite:
Mono Lake Sunset

MAMMOTH LAKES

Mammoth Lakes is, today, by far one of the most popular ski resorts in California, especially for Angelenos, as it is easy to get to from L. A. For S.F. Bay Area folks, Kirkwood and Lake Tahoe are more within reach. There are three parts to the town of **Mammoth Lakes**, other than the very much developed town itself: Mammoth Mountain, Mammoth Lakes and the Devils Postpile/Rainbow Falls area.

From June Lake, drive to the June Lake Junction and turn right on US 395. It is a fast 15 to 20 miles to Mammoth Lakes. After a few of miles on US 395 notice a sign that says **Deadman Summit**. There is nothing to worry about - you are on a fast paved road in a nice car in the 21st century. The name dates back from the Gold Rush days. Nearby they found the head of a dead man in a whisky barrel.

Opposite: Devils Postpile National Monument

Five miles before the turnoff to State Route 203 taking you into the town of Mammoth Lakes, is the turnoff for the **Mammoth Scenic route**.

If you plan to go to the Mountain or Devils Postpile area, turn right; if not, or of this your first visit, keep going. Turn right on SR 203, the main road in town.

As you enter town, there is the **Welcome Center** on your right. Make a stop there first. Check out the books of local interest and get some up to date information on campgrounds, lodging and the road to Devils Postpile from the Park Ranger and the friendly volunteers that work there.

They carry a free newspaper with very useful information, not just on Mammoth, but the entire Eastern Sierra.

History

Just like any spot in the region, the first men came here as a result of the Gold Rush, but roughly 30 years later. In 1875 four prospectors discovered a promising quartz outcrop. Soon the town of Mammoth City was born. It went through all the typical phases of a Gold Mining town: houses and schools were built, people moved in, every once and a while disaster struck (fire) and eventually, unlike other places, Mammoth City did not recover from it. But it was on the map for good. Eventually, people realized that Mammoth Mountain, 11,053 ft., could be great for skiing.

In 1941, a Mr. Mc Coy obtained a permit to operate his own portable rope, powered by a Ford Model "A" engine. This was most certainly the predecessor of the ski lift.

Mammoth Lakes

Take Lake Mary road, the extension of SR 203, the main road, to get to the lakes area. The first set of lakes is **Twin Lakes**, with **Lake Mary** and **Lake Mamie** to follow. If you take a left turn towards Lake Mary you can also get to **Lake George**. There are many beautiful and easy hikes in this area. I am only mentioning a few. Several booklets with Easy Day Hikes are available at the Mammoth Lakes Welcome Center. This is how I found out about these walks.

TJ Lake and Lake Barrett

Drive to Lake George, park and walk through the campground. You will face the trail head on the other side, have to cross a small stream climb uphill for a bit but after that it is all beautiful pine trees and an easy walk. The entire walk is less than two miles and you will reach two beautiful lakes. Note however that you may not find the trail above the rocks early in the season because of snow. That was my first experience, even thought it was already June. After all, the Mammoth Lakes area is above 8,000 ft.

Lake Mamie

Today there are ski lifts, gondolas, etc. When the ski season finally ends, the mountain biking one takes over. The same slopes are used for bike riders, the most challenging trail being called the **Kamikaze Trail** !

As mentioned earlier, there are different parts of Mammoth Lakes that are of interest to visitors: the lakes area, the mountain itself and the Devils Postpile area.

Emerald Lake

This is probably the easiest hike in the entire Eastern Sierra. To get to the trail head, drive to the other end of Lake Mary and then through the Coldwater campground. Make sure you get past the campground itself. There is another parking lot with two trail heads, one for **Crystal Lake** and one for **Emerald Lake**. An easy one mile

Emerald Lake

stroll will take you to Emerald lake, where you have a great view of the **Mammoth Crest**.

Mammoth Mountain

I grew up in a flat country, so I do not have the skiing in me. One thing to do however that does not require skis, just $16, is to take the gondola at the **Mammoth Mountain Inn**. Take a right turn on the corner of main street and Minaret road, or a right turn towards Mammoth Mountain if you took the scenic road. Buy a ticket for the gondola at the Inn and take the ride all the way to the top. You will have a 360 degree view of the entire area.

Just make sure you are wearing proper clothing. After all, you will be at 11,053 ft. Walk slowly, so the altitude does not get to you. And it will be windy up there.

Minaret Vista

From the top of Mammoth Mountain, looking north to northwest, you can see an interesting structure, called the **Minarets**. You can even notice them from US 395 when you drive by the Mammoth airport, going north. The

best view, with a nice, easy nature trail to go with it, is from, guess what, the Minaret Vista point. This is further up the road from the Mammoth Mountain Inn and also as far as they will let you drive: the Minaret Vista parking lot. Drive back down to the ski area if you want to go to Devils Postpile.

Rainbow Falls and Devils Postpile

This is another must see in the Eastern Sierra. I am calling it a freak of nature. The **Devils Postpile** area is actually located on the west side of the Sierra Nevada mountain range. The road from Mammoth Mountain crosses he Sierra Crest and leads to many trail heads.

Gondola arriving at the summit

When you take the gondola to the top of Mammoth Mountain, you have great views in all directions

As parts of the road are single lane and to protect the environment, driving in there is not permitted, except for very early in the morning. Instead, you need to take a mandatory shuttle.

Tickets can be bought and the shuttle taken at the Mammoth Mountain Inn, the same spot where the gondola leaves. The advantage to all this: you can get off and on where you like, all

of that for $7. What I recommend is to take the shuttle, get off at **Reds Meadow,** walk down (1 1/2 mile) to **Rainbow Falls** and from there walk to Devils Postpile, then wait for the shuttle to go back. 90% of the people get off at Devils Postpile, walk to Rainbow Falls and climb 1 1/4 mile uphill to the Reds Meadow stop. I asked the bus driver, as I was the only person left on the bus after the Devils Postpile stop, about it and she agreed.

There are several other shuttle stops, including Sotcher Lake which has a nice, easy, flat nature trail going around that lake.

From the Reds Meadow stop walk down to Rainbow Falls. Here you are on the west side of the Sierra Nevada looking at the San Joaquin River. The spot is called Rainbow Falls because most days, in particular around noon, you will see a rainbow. I have not been very successful in capturing a spectacular one, but there always was a little bit of a rainbow when I went there.

The walk down and the relatively flat trail towards Devils Postpile goes through a forest that was subject to a big fire in, I believe, 1994. Because of that there is no natural canape and it can be hot in the summer time. Wear a hat or baseball cap.

When you reach Devils Postpile, the path will merge with the **John Muir Trail**.

Minarets as seen from the summit of Mammoth Mountain

We will run into this trail again in this book. The area you are now walking in is actually a National Monument.

Devils Postpile itself is an unusual formation of tall columns of molten basalt, that solidified thousands

Rainbow Falls. There should always be a rainbow in the middle of the day.

Before returning to June Lake it might be a good idea to do some grocery shopping or have a small bite to eat.

Along Old Mammoth Road, south of Main Street, is a big square with businesses, including a nice Photo Gallery, banks and a Vons. Vons is to Southern California what Safeways is in Northern California, a large grocery store chain.

There is also no shortage of places to eat. One restaurant I always like to go for a beer is **Whiskey Creek**, on the corner of Lake Mary road and Minaret road. It is the home of the **Mammoth Brewing Company**. *"A brewery with an altitude"* is their slogan. They make excellent ales. Whiskey Creek opens every day at 5 p.m. and has happy hour beer prices until 6.30pm. During that time everything on the food menu is half price. The brewery is upstairs, the bigger dining room downstairs.

Next door to the Mammoth Mountain Inn is another interesting place called the **Jodler,** where the Mammoth beer is served. They have great burgers and you can sit outside on the deck and watch the gondola go up and down.

Opposite: Other view of Devils Postpile

of years ago and formed columns. There is a short trail to the top of the Postpile. Notice that they are shaped like perfect hexagons. The columns broke down at the bottom. Do not climb on these rocks!

A short five minute walk will take you to the shuttle stop. There you find rest rooms and a Ranger Station where you can pick up a brochure as a souvenir.

Food and Lodging

As you can see when driving through the town, and checking all the flyers available at the Welcome Center, there are many places to stay in Mammoth Lakes. Some of those even have names making you think you are in Switzerland, *Alpenhof* for example. As you probably left your suitcase in June Lake you may not need lodging.

VI

TIOGA PASS

t 9,945 ft. this is the highest auto pass in California. It also marks the entrance of Yosemite National Park. On average it is open 166 days a year. In Chapter Two I explained why this pass is closed for such a long period of time and how to find out when it opens.

Often the road towards the park from US 395 opens before the section inside the Yosemite does. In this chapter we visit interesting spots located outside the Park itself. In the next chapter we explore the **Yosemite High Country** inside the Park.

From June Lake it is a short drive to **Tioga Pass**. You can either go around the loop or straight to the June Lake junction and then turn left on US 395, which is faster. Fill the tank, if needed. After about 10 miles, just before the town of Lee Vining is the turnoff for

Tioga Pass. Turn left onto SR 120, the Tioga Road. By now you should have seen at least two signs telling you whether the pass is open or not. On the left side of the road is the **Mobil station**, that doubles as the local gourmet food attraction: lobster taquitos at a gas station!

After five miles you pass the gate that is closed in winter. The next six miles you climb 3000 vertical feet, going through **Lee Vining Canyon**.

Notice how there is nothing growing on the right hand side of the road. Watch out for rocks! This part of the road, called **Blue Slide**, is dangerous during a thunderstorm or heavy rain. Do not drive here in severe weather conditions.

The road then curves to the left. There are a few pullouts where you can stop

and look back east: you can see the Mono Craters, Mono Lake and mountains in Nevada in the far distance. After one turn to the right you will reach **Ellery Lake**. The road curves around Ellery Lake and continues on towards the Park. As you drive on you will notice a large parking lot on your right marked **Nunatak Nature Trail**.

This is a great opportunity to stretch your legs for 15 minutes by walking this trail and look at the educational and informative displays along it. A **nunatak** is an area, like the top of **Mount Dana**, the peak you see on the left side of the road, that remained free of ice in the midst of the surrounding glaciers during the Ice Period.

A little further up the road there is a turnoff to the right. A short paved road will lead to a parking lot near a bridge across Mill Creek. Next to it is

Opposite: Tioga Lake, still covered with patches of ice. Some years it is still like this in the first week of July

Tioga Road, east of the pass. This section is called Blue Slide. A 3000 ft. drop in six miles.

a dirt road, that, when it is open, can take us to **Saddlebag Lake**.

We will come back to this spot but first drive to Tioga Pass itself. The road curves along the Tioga Pass Resort and then opens up for a great view of **Tioga Lake**. It now makes its final ascent and as you approach the Park, turn around by the upper Tioga Lake vista point. We will cover 20 miles of the inner part of the Park in the next chapter.

In this chapter I walk you through a few areas just outside the Park. The walk to **Bennettville** and the **Twenty Lakes Area** on the other side of Saddlebag Lake are some of my all-time favorites.

Early on in the season, when Tioga Pass is not yet open, but the gate five miles from US 395 is, there may be nice weather so you can do some of the walks described here. The water taxi across Saddlebag Lake will not yet be available though.

History of Tioga Pass

This should not be a surprise but the first road to Tioga Pass was established because of mining and the Gold

st of the Pass - Memorial Day

Rush, or should I say Silver Rush? In 1881 the **Great Consolidated Silver Company** was established and they built mining camps along what is now Tioga Pass: the Tioga Mine and Bennettville. This was before Yosemite National Park was created.

formation kiosk - Tioga Overlook- Memorial Day

Shell Lake, one of the many lakes beyond Bennettville

A road was needed to reach the mines from Big Oak Flat, and became the **Great Sierra Wagon Trail**. When the road was completed in 1883, the Tioga Mine itself was already closed.

The word "**Tiog**a" is Iroquois, not Paiute, and means **"where it forks"**. East Coast prospectors probably chose this name. The Tioga road is west-east.

For a very long time there was no road from Mono Lake to Tioga Pass.. Not until 1909 was there a road coming from the east side. It was a good road for automobiles, although before 1913 no one could legally enter Yosemite by car. Once this was legal, there was more traffic in the park, creating a need to widen and reroute the Tioga Road. The road, as we know it today, was opened on June 24 of 1961.

Bennettville

An adorable walk, with a little bit of history to think of, is the walk to

Bennettville. You can reach a couple of lakes further up the trail. Park near the Junction Meadow Campground, which we mentioned earlier, right before the Saddlebag Road. If no spots are available, find suitable parking along Tioga Road. Do not park at the campground. These spaces are for paying campers.

Cross the bridge. You will see a large bulletin board with a map of the area and a hiker's sign-in register (sign in!). This is the trail head. The trail will go through switchbacks above the campground, take you into a lodge pole pine forest and follow Mine Creek.

Note that all the creeks encountered in this chapter, Mill, Slater, Saddlebag and Tioga, eventually merge into Lee

Restored building at Bennettville

Vining Creek and that a lot of its water will not reach Mono Lake, but: Los Angeles. In the next chapter, all the bodies of water we encounter are a water source for: San Francisco. What a difference a mile makes!

After passing a small gorge where Mill Creek turns into a waterfall you will reach the site of the old mining town of Bennettville. The two buildings were restored in 1993 by the Forest Service, trying to match the originals of around 1880. Just imagine what it was like living here in 1881: no real road, no real anything, but maybe I will find silver tomorrow ?

If you decide to move on, follow the trail for another five minutes until it forks: swing right. The easy trail, following Mill Creek, will take you to several lakes: **Shell**, **Mine**, **Fantail** and **Spuller Lake**. Turn around when you feel like it - just enjoy the walk and the backdrop of Mount Dana on your return.

Depending on which time of the year you are taking this walk, there may be some negotiating between getting your feet wet or climbing on a few rocks, to get to the first or second lake, but it is mostly fun. All I got out of it were wet socks!

Saddlebag Lake and the Twenty Lakes Area

I consider this by far the most amazing place in the entire Eastern Sierra, if the time is right. The road to Saddlebag Lake usually opens two weeks after Tioga Pass does, but that is just the road itself. Then the Saddlebag Lake Resort opens a week or two after that. Saddlebag Lake has an elevation of 10,087 ft. To give you an example, in 2006 Tioga Pass opened on June 17, but the road to Saddlebag only after 4th of July. The only picture I could take was one of the parking lot covered with snow. The water taxi was still weeks away. Once it is available, it operates until September 30th.

Don't let the words Saddlebag Resort fool you: it is a place where you can have a burger or a sandwich, pay for a spot on the campground and, most importantly, buy a ticket for the water taxi.

To get there, from the Junction Meadow parking lot off Tioga Road, is to take the mostly dirt road for two miles to get to the Resort. Park near the Resort or at the overflow parking. The superb attraction of the water taxi is that you can, for $10, be taken to

...sco Lake - My personal favorite picture of 2006. I sat down on a rock, took another picture: Voila!

the other side of the lake, tell them when you want to be picked up, adding some sense of security that they might be looking for you if you do not show up for the return, and

cut 45 minutes each way out of your hiking time.

You can walk around the lake if the taxi is not operating, but the hike and

the scenery is nothing compared to what is waiting for you on the other side. This is one of those few locations where you can drive to, and water taxi to, a beautiful spot that is way above

Steelhead Lake - July 18 2005

This gives you plenty of time to stop, relax, admire the view and take pictures.

The first half of the loop will take you past **Hummingbird Lake** and then you will have to walk down on slate rocks for a while from **Odell Lake** to **Helen Lake**.

From Helen Lake there is a trail, an old mining road of course, going all the way down to Lundy Canyon, which is almost 2000 ft. lower.

I would love to do this hike one day but this requires, at a minimum, one hiking buddy and two cars, as the trail head on the other end is more than 20 miles from Saddlebag. Instead walk over the logs crossing the outlet of Helen Lake and follow the trail around the lake. You will have to walk over a ridge, possibly some patches of snow

10,000ft. Then you can walk for miles with virtually no elevation gain. The area on the other side of the lake is called the **Twenty Lakes Basin** The best map for this is the (free) menu of the Saddlebag Lake Resort and it shows you many choices for a great hiking experience. I am describing only a few. All these trails are there because they are old mining roads.

Twenty Lakes Basin Loop

Once you get to the other side of the lake, there are, as the name suggests, some twenty or so lakes, at a similar elevation, 10,300 ft., waiting for your enjoyment. If you do not feel like hiking five miles at above 10,000 feet, I recommend you take the left half of the loop, which takes you to Steelhead Lake, passing a few lakes on the way. Except for the first 20 minutes, the trail is mostly flat.

If you want to hike the entire loop I recommend a counter-clockwise approach. Ask the folks on the water taxi about conditions on the trail.

Plan at least four hours when you schedule your water taxi return time.

The water taxi

(brought your hiking poles?) and then you reach **Shamrock Lake**.

The view in either direction is magnificent. And just remember that less than two hours ago you were still inside your car. Where else in the world can you do this?

The trail goes over one more ridge along **Excelsior Lake** and then takes you down to Steelhead Lake, where you need to cross its inlet. A possible side tour to your right is to the site of an old Tungsten Mine.

The remainder of the loop is easy and mostly downhill. You pass Wasco and Greenstone Lake back to Saddlebag to catch your water taxi. In the summer time, you will find an abundance of wildflowers along that section of the trail, so if it is too early for your taxi, admire those wildflowers and take lots of pictures. Once you get to the dock there will be an abundance of mosquitoes so bring insect repellent.

Conness Lake

Along the west side of the loop I just described, there are two peaks that dominate the landscape: **North Peak** (12,242 ft.) and **Mt. Conness** (12,590

Wasco Lake in July of 2005

ft.) In front of Mt. Conness is Conness Glacier. There are some lakes at the bottom of that glacier, surprisingly called Conness Lakes.

Mountain, glacier and lakes are named after John Conness who was an Irish-born California senator from 1863 until 1869.

If you like the Saddlebag water taxi and the Twenty Lakes Basin as much as I do and want to go back, Conness Lake is another four hour gem of a walk. It is the only hike in the book without a well marked trail.

There are different ways to get to Conness Lake, one more beautiful than the other. Just make sure someone knows where you are. I describe the most traveled trail here.

Start with the left hand side of the loop until you are almost past the first lake, Greenstone Lake. Follow the trail around the lake and listen to the sound of a waterfall, in case you lose the trail. After a short cross country walk you should pick up a trail that goes along a stream, which is the inlet to Greenstone Lake.

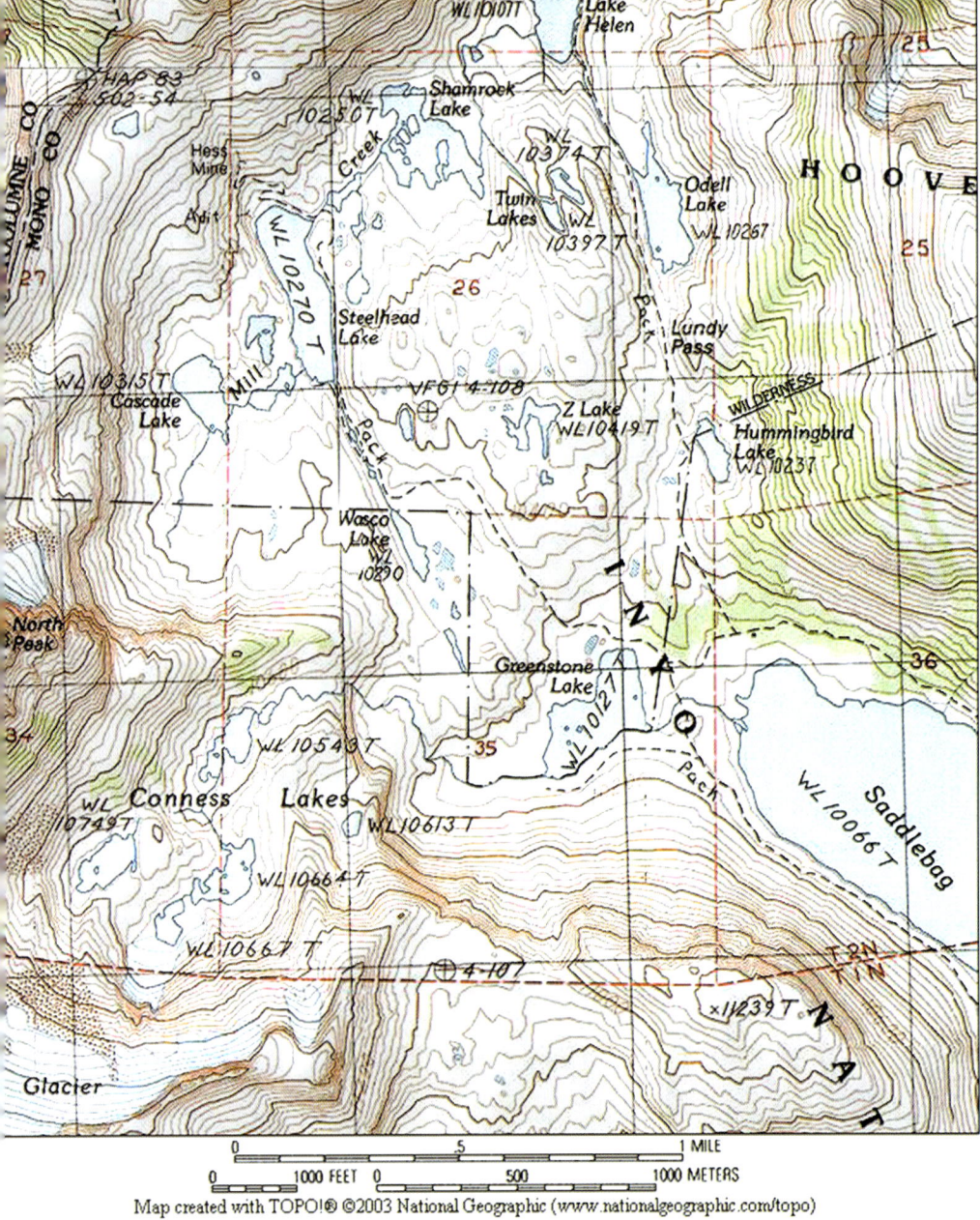

Twenty Lakes Basin - Topographic map of the region

Once the stream curves you should see the waterfall and now you will have to walk uphill on granite. This is easier than it seems, just pace yourself because of the altitude. You need to get to above the waterfall, which will be easy if there are not too many patches of snow, or mosquitoes.

Now you see the stream that feeds the waterfall and are in the flat meadow with the glacier right in front of you. If you walk towards the glacier you will reach the first of the Conness lakes. The color of its water as almost turquoise.

Do not forget to, both on your way up and down, stop many times to admire the landscape looking towards both Steelhead and Saddlebag Lake. Quite unique and breathtaking it is.

A different way, but more of a trial and error path is to first walk towards Wasco Lake, turn around it counterclockwise and then climb the ridge.

The guy from the water taxi told me about it. He does it in 35 minutes. I needed three hours as there was more error than trial here. But every step, every mile, every climb on a rock was beautiful and worth it!

nness Lake

Potter Lake and Cascade Lake

A nice alternative, if there is not much time, is the walk to **Potter Lake** and **Cascade Lake.** Space on the water taxi is limited to about a dozen people so the return time of your choice may not be available. There is a taxi every half hour. So if you do not have enough time, or do not want to walk around Saddlebag Lake, this is the walk to take. From the place where the water taxi drops you off take the left side of the loop. Follow the trail and pass Greenstone and Wasco lakes. As you approach Steelhead Lake, take the narrower trail to the left. It goes slowly uphill, then swings left just before the lake. After a few switchbacks the trail faces the direction you came from. Do not continue on it, as it is another trail to Conness Lake. Instead, take the path to the right. **Potter Lake** is right there. At the lake you have great views of Steelhead Lake and beyond, North Peak and Mount Conness.

Cascade Lake is not far away. You can reach it by walking over granite or by following the trail on the other side of Potter Lake. This trail goes all the way to **Secret Lake** but that would require more time.

View from Potter Lake - Cascade Lake and North Peak

Slate Creek Valley

There is another great walk in the area. It is a great choice late in the season when there is no water taxi but the road to Saddlebag Lake is still open.

This hike requires crossing Saddlebag Creek. Its difficulty depends on the time of year and how much snowfall there was that year. I did this one in October and had no problem. I also was the only person on the trail. To get to the trail head, take the road towards Saddlebag Lake and turn left at the

Sawmill Campground parking lot. In October the campground itself is closed for the season but you can still park there and walk into it.

Go straight through the campground. Do not get confused by the small trails that lead to the campsites, follow the main trail. As you leave the campsite it climbs and then curves to the left. This is where you have to cross Saddlebag Creek. When I did so there was even a tree across the stream to walk on and the runoff of Saddlebag Lake was reasonable slow. Once across the creek

you go through a forest and enter **Hall Natural Area**. It is used for ecological research. About twenty minutes later you will see the remains of a building used for research.

From that point forward you are in Slate Creek Valley and you can just keep walking until you feel like returning to the trail head. You will approach **Coyote Ridge** and can start climbing, realizing that there should be another way to get to Conness Lakes.

Great view from the trail in Slate Creek Valley

Instead you can just relax, enjoy the view and the mountain air. Return to the campground the same way you came. As you drive back towards Lee Vining this may be the right opportunity to have a bite to eat at the famous Mobil Station. The deli part is actually called **The Whoa Nellie Deli** and the chef calls himself **Tioga Toomey.** They recently changed their menu. It all looks "jammie".

VII

TIOGA ROAD

In this chapter, I take you inside Yosemite National Park, over Tioga Pass, All the spots and walks are along the first 20 miles of the Tioga Road. Drive to Tioga Pass, following the directions listed in the previous chapter. Pay the entrance fee ($25), show your receipt from less than seven days ago or your **National Parks and Federal Recreation Lands Pass** at the gate. This pass latter replaces the National Parks Pass, costs $80 and is valid for a year.

Yosemite Valley itself is almost 100 miles from June Lake. Driving all the way to the Valley, spending enough time there and then driving back, all in one day, would not make for a nice comfortable day trip. Visit the Valley as part of a trip to or from one of the Gold Country destinations instead. All the must see spots in Yosemite Valley are listed in Chapter Thirteen.

The stretch of Tioga Road covered in this chapter is between the Park entrance and the **Olmsted Point** vista point, about 20 miles.

This part of the park is the **Yosemite High Country** and dominated by the **Tuolemne Meadows** Area. An indispensable tool to visit this wonderland is the "**Map & Guide to Tuolemne Meadows**" available from the Yosemite Association. It costs $2.95 and covers the area mentioned in the previous chapter as well. Most Visitor Centers as well as the Mono Lake Committee carry it.

This overview lists my favorite walks, hikes and spots to take pictures. You can also simply relax on an ancient piece of granite rock and imagine what it was like a mere 150 years ago when **Chief Tenaya** and his tribe followed the **Mono Trail** here.

Gaylor Lakes

As soon as you enter the Park, turn right into the small parking lot. This is where the trail head for **Gaylor Lakes** is. Across the road you can see Mount Dana. I first decided to hike Gaylor Lakes because it is so short. I noticed on a Yosemite map it was only one mile and thought I was in for an easy one hour stroll. That part, however, is deceiving. Making it up to Gaylor Pass means 1,000 ft. elevation gain in that one mile. However, every foot will be rewarded at the top.

So do not give up, stop along the way, take pictures, drink your water and walk your way up. In part this means stepping on rocks that somebody put there for you over a 100 years ago, turning the trail into a natural stairway almost.

Opposite: Different view of Half Dome from the Nature Trail at Olmsted Point

View from Gaylor Pass in July

Lyell fork of the Tuolumne River

Once you are inside Yosemite National Park itself, you will notice a stream on the left hand side of the road. That is the **Tuolumne River**. About six miles into the Park are a couple of signs and a turnoff on the left, marked Tuolumne Lodge, with a large parking lot.

If you like to try a nice section of the John Muir Trail, this is the place to do it. It is the easiest walk in the entire book. Pick up the trail at the parking lot. The John Muir Trail (JMT) itself is hundreds of miles long, ends at Mt. Whitney and is for backpackers. This section is an easy walk.

In this part where you pick up the JMT it actually consists of multiple, parallel trails, sometimes compared to a freeway for hikers. You walk through a meadow, with nice wildflowers in season, then approach pine trees when you get closer to the stream.

Turn right to cross the bridge over the river and then turn left. Soon you will see a billboard with a display of local nature features and a map. This is where the trail forks.

Each time you stop, look back towards Mount Dana and the Tioga Road. You will see many mini-lakes across the

Same view Labor Day weekend

road. Once you reach the crest, the trail takes you down to Gaylor Lakes and the terrain changes into cross country. You can either turn back or walk around and enjoy the view. All depends on what time of the year you are doing this.

As you can tell from the photographs of Gaylor Lakes - Upper, Lower and Middle Gaylor Lakes was just some big pack of ice in early July one year! Either way, from the crest the view is magnificent, only one mile away from your car !

ll Fork of the Tuolemne River

Turn right. After an easy 15 minute stroll you will reach the Lyell fork of the Tuolumne river, not the Dana fork, which you already crossed. Admire the great views looking east. There is another bridge with a narrow trail on your left on the other side of the stream.

However, to catch the continuation of the JMT, you need to continue on straight for about one quarter of a mile until you see the John Muir Trail sign and then take a left. Walk as far as you like.

The trail is all flat and easy, despite the 9,000 ft. altitude. Admire the different colors of the water ranging from blue to turquoise and the polished granite rocks it flows over!

Tuolumne Meadows

It is rare to find a very large, green meadow at an elevation of 8,600 ft. The runoff from the surrounding mountains does find its way into streams, but much of it also seeps underground. This explains why trees do not grow in Tuolemne Meadows.

Tuolumne Meadows is located about eight miles into the Park from the east entrance. Crossing the bridge across the Tuolumne River marks the beginning of the Meadows. It is about twelve miles long. It is very wet during the first few weeks it can be reached. Then the snow melts and dumps the water into the Lyell and Dana forks of what will eventually become the Tuolumne River.

The Mono Trail, a trans-Sierra route, goes right through the Meadows. Miwok Indians in the west trading with Mono Indians used that trail for a very long time. It goes from what is now Yosemite Valley, passes **Tenaya Lake** and goes over the Sierra Crest at **Mono Pass**. There it goes down **Bloody Canyon** all the way to Mono Lake. There is a Mono Pass trail head along Tioga Road.

Tuolumne Meadows with deer

Tuolemne Meadows near Soda Springs

There is a trail head as well. Walk on a service road first that takes you to the main trail and into Tuolemne Meadows by **Parsons Memorial Lodge** and Soda Springs.

Parsons lodge was created by the Sierra Club. They decided to create a lodge at Soda Springs as a meeting place, reading room and mountain headquarters. They also decided to dedicate it to **Edward Parsons**, a Sierra Club member who organized excursions in the area. In the same year it was decided to name a trail after yet another Sierra Cllub member, John Muir: the John Muir Trail. That took several years to be complete (1938), but the lodge was built in 1915.

I would not recommend taking it all the way through Bloody Canyon. After all, it was named like this because of all the blood on the rocks from horses who did not survive the trip down.

Today, Tuolemne Meadows is a very popular part of Yosemite. There is a Visitor Center, open until mid September. The campground there is extremely popular, so most times it is either closed or full. Check way in advance. A few weeks later all is quiet and there may be almost no water left in the river itself. A few weeks after that, the road closes and Tuolemne Meadows cannot be reached until next year.

There are several nice walks and hikes starting in Tuolemne Meadows.

First Visit to the Meadows

A nice walk through the Meadows is always relaxing, finding a parking spot may not be. Therefor, I recommend turning right just before the bridge that crosses the river, marked as the Lembert Dome parking lot,

Drive all the way to the end of the road until it turns right. There you find another parking lot near some stables. Park there.

Parsons Lodge

Tenaya Lake

Our next stop is Tenaya Lake. The lake is named after chief Tenaya, a native American Indian who's father was the chief of the Ahwahneechee, the peoples that lived in Yosemite Valley.

Tenaya grew up with the Mono Indians though. There was a constant conflict between him, his tribe, and the white men, about sending them to a Reservation near Fresno or staying in Yosemite.

On the west side of the lake is a small beach. You can reach it from the road or from a parking lot just 50 yards before it. I always like to close my eyes, while being on that beach, and imagine that, as soon as I open them, I would go back in time and see the people that used to live there.

The sand of the beach seems to have glittering ore in it. Probably not gold at all, sorry. If the time of the year is right, and mosquitoes have taken the day off, get your feet wet or go for a swim.

There is a trail around the lake you can reach by crossing an inlet near the end of the beach. It is a very nice walk.

Boat in Tenaya lake as seen from the trail that goes around the lake

The lodge still exists today, has some nice displays and very friendly people welcoming you on your visit. It even acts as a shelter when sudden thunderstorms hit Tuolemne Meadows. Nearby Soda Springs is very unique as the natural spring contains so much Sodium, as well as Calcium and CO_2.

Glen Aulin Trail

The nice folks at the Visitor Center suggested this trail when I told them I was looking for something easy for my first day. On a first day of a trip it is always recommended to allow your body to adjust to the altitude.

You can pick up the trail behind Parsons Lodge. Do not follow the service road closer to the river (After about a mile, you will encounter a sign that reads: **This is not the Glen Aulin Trail**). From there you first meander through the Meadows, then walk through a forest. There is almost no elevation gain if you walk only a few miles as I did. Just walk as long as you feel like and then turn back.

Tenaya Lake with Mount Conness as seen from the Sunrise trailhead

The only downside is that you have to make a choice between returning the same way or walk a mile along the paved SR 120.

On the east side of the lake there is another parking lot with rest rooms. It is a popular spot for a picnic. Why not? An even nicer spot is at the end of the lake, at the Sunrise trail head.

Olmsted Point

Not far from Tenaya Lake you reach a large parking lot, marked as Olmsted Point. It is named after **Frederick Law**

Olmsted, who saw Yosemite for the first time in 1864. He was an outdoor architect, mostly known for designing Central Park in New York and many campuses, including the Stanford University Campus, which I adore.

Olmsted Point is one of my favorite spots to make a stop. A lot of people do so, then get out of their car, take pictures of Half Dome, which you can see from there, and then get back into the car and drive on.

The secret: there is a five minute walk from that very parking lot that puts you away from the crowd and on top

of granite domes facing Half Dome and Clouds Rest. Simply walk down from the parking lot on what looks like a stairway that was built just for you. Notice the fossils on some of the rocks.

Less than five minutes later you will walk on granite, admire a great view of Half Dome and feel like you are surrounded only by peace and silence.

Once you are done admiring or photographing the view of Half Dome, turn back and walk up the granite structure until you get to a spot where you can see Tenaya Lake and all the domes in the background. Ansel Adams must have taken one of his photographs from the very same spot.

This is as far as this chapter takes us into Yosemite National Park. There is still time needed to get back over Tioga Pass. In Chapter 13, the highlights of Yosemite Valley are covered.

Opposite:
Tenaya Lake from Olmsted Point

VIII

MAMMOTH TO BISHOP

Drive to the, by now familiar, June Lake junction and turn right on US 395. It is about 55 miles from June Lake to **Bishop**, the largest town in Inyo County. There are several interesting places along the way. This makes for a very nice day trip. Simply select which place you want to visit.

Convict Lake

About 5 miles south of the junction with SR 203, the Mammoth Lakes junction, there is a turnoff to take you to **Convict Lake**. When you reach the lake, turn left and look for a parking spot.

There is an interesting double history to this lake. In 1871, when the lake and canyon were still called Monte Diablo, 29 prisoners escaped from a jail in Carson City, NV. They were chased down by a posse led by sheriff Robert Morrison, who eventually got killed in the adventure. The lake was renamed Convict Lake because of that and the highest mountain behind it is now **Mt. Morrison**.

More than 100 years later, children were playing on the frozen lake and fell through it. Several men came to the rescue and all the children were safe but two of the men died.

I met people who actually knew the ones that perished, so I am not mentioning any names. A nice commemorative plaque explaining the story can be found right in front of the lake.

There is a very nice walk you can take around the lake. If you parked on the left side of the lake you can find the trail head at the end of that parking lot. Check the beach area first to take a picture of **Mt. Laurel** and Mt. Morrison. This spot and trail is particularly beautiful in the fall when all the leaves are turning.

The complete walk is only two miles, with almost no elevation gain. At the western end of the lake, where it has its inlet, a wooden walkway was built so you do not have to get your feet wet, or have to turn back because of too much water.

This is very nice. When I did the walk, in the fall of 2005, the stream was still flowing over the walkway. But all the kids loved it.

Tom's Place and Rock Creek Canyon

This is by far the most exciting walk you can take in the entire Eastern Sierra and is not strenuous at all. The only hike that competes with it, is

Opposite: Convict Lake and Mount Morrison

A lovely walk awaits you

the Twenty Lakes Area Loop above Saddlebag Lake, which I mentioned in the Tioga Pass chapter. Try both so you can decide which one is your favorite.

What both have in common is that the starting point is above 10,000 ft. - higher than Tioga Pass - and both trail heads can be reached by automobile.

Continuing south on US 395, take the **Tom's Place** exit and drive nine miles through **Rock Creek Canyon**. If you are visiting in the fall you may want to stop a few times along the way, as Rock Creek Canyon is one of the superb canyons for fall colors. The very end of the paved road, which passes Rock Creek Lake, takes you to the trail head. It is called **Mosquito Flat** (10,300 ft.).

In the summer time that name should be a gentle reminder to carry insect repellent with you.

From the trail head, start walking and soon you see a sign telling you that you are entering the **John Muir Wilderness** Area. Most places that I am taking you to are not inside a National Park, but inside a Wilderness Area named after famous people or, sometimes, no people at all, like the **Golden Trout Wilderness** Area. The good news is, all these are protected land.

As you follow Rock Creek, the trail goes uphill for a little bit but after half

a mile, the worst part is over. From this moment on you have entered **Little Lakes Valley** and the trail will just go up and down, nice and easy.

In the summertime you will see wildflowers everywhere. The trail itself, is, not surprisingly, an old mining road. It goes all the way up to Morgan Pass (11,104 ft.). I usually turn back when I get to **Long Lake** (10,543 ft.) You need to cross a stream before getting to Long Lake, but there are rocks to step on.

Assume three miles each way for the walk to Long Lake. Do it at your own

Rock Creek Lake, which you will pass to get to the Mosquito Flat trail head

ck Creek meets the trail on the way to Long Lake

pace, to most this will be a four hour round trip. As you return to US 395, do not hesitate to stop at Tom's Place, right before the highway. It was originally built in 1917 then purchased by Thomas Jefferson Yerby and his wife in 1923. This is how it got its name. There is a saloon and a restaurant on one side of the street that parallels US 395. There is lodging across the street. Inside the saloon there are some very interesting artefacts hanging against the wall, several suggesting this is another *ECV* watering hole . Also interesting is one of the beers they

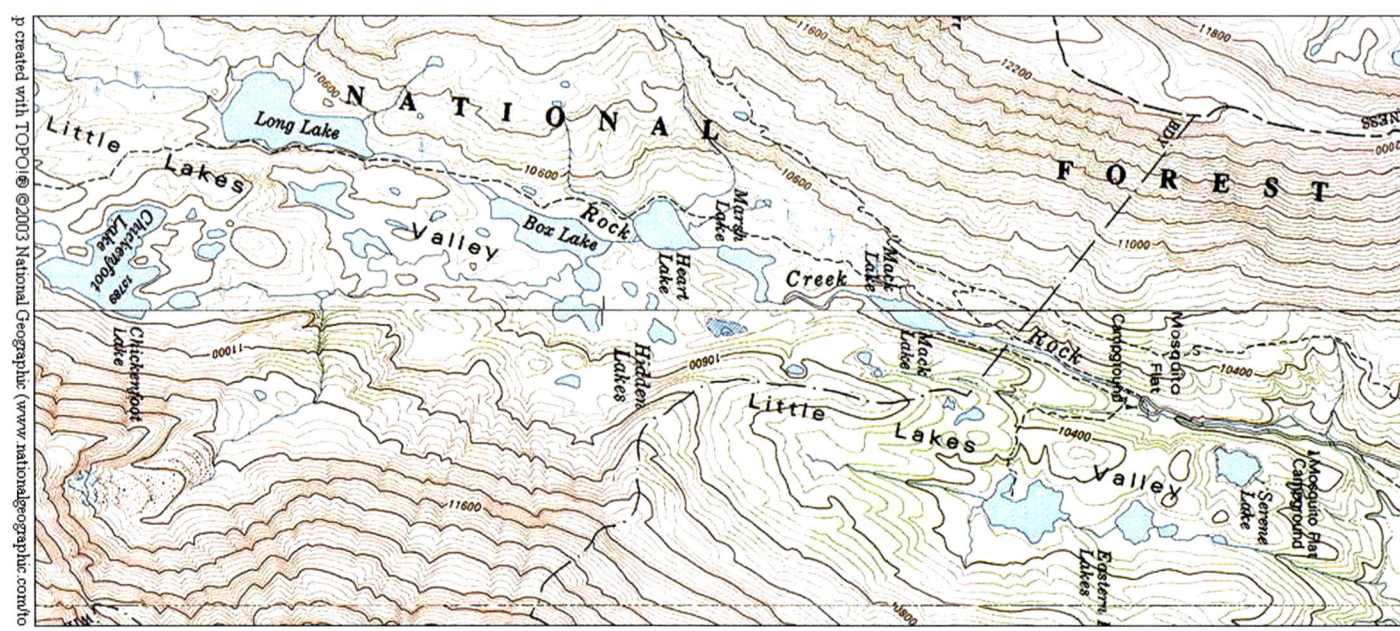

Little Lakes Valley from Mosquito Flat to Long Lake - A wonderful walk at above 10,000 ft.

serve there, Toms Brew, an orange flavored beer brewed in the Mojave desert. It is actually very refreshing after a healthy walk in Little Lakes Valley.

Bishop Creek Canyon

Now we are on our way to the town of Bishop. US 395 drops down from Tom's Place with great views of the Sierra Crest on your right, including **Mount Tom**. If you are visiting in the fall, a detour to **Bishop Creek Canyon** is highly recommended.

To do so, look for a sign showing Ed Powers road, then turn right. This will allow you to get there without entering Bishop itself first and take you to the continuation of West Line Street, a few miles closer to the mountains.

Notice the interesting rock formations surrounding you. This area is called the **Buttermilk**, popular amongst rock climbers and mountain bikers. The road will curve a few times and gain elevation. A look back shows some dramatic views of the valley, the town of Bishop and the White Mountains

across from it. The road continues and takes you to several turnoffs, going to **South lake**, **North Lake** or **Lake Sabrina** All these lakes display beautiful backdrops to the back country and have trail heads to many hours of beautiful hiking.

Past the turnoff of South Like, you reach the small community of **Aspendell.** It is a charming little place and also the end of the road in the winter time. If you continue, in the fall , you will see glowing aspen trees everywhere. Less than one mile before Lake

Sabrina, the true end of the road in summer and fall .are some great spots for fall color picture taking.

One fall, I drove up to Bishop Creek Canyon, from June lake, to take fall color pictures. There are a few bridges crossing the creek near Lake Sabrina and I remembered just the spot. I noticed a van and a photographer with a view camera. It was **Verne Clevenger**, of Bishop. I mention his gallery later in this chapter. I decided not to disturb him and made the trip a second time the next day. As it turns out, I had better light.

Bishop Pass - Long Lake

As I mentioned, there are several trails leading you from any of those three lakes into the back country. My favorite one was recommended to me by a friendly guide at the Mammoth Welcome Center.

It leaves at South Lake and can take you across **Bishop Pass** into King's Canyon National Park. I only went as far as beautiful **Long Lake**, a different Long Lake than the one in Rock Creek Canyon. Even though the elevation of the town of Bishop is just above 5,000

Bishop Creek near Lake Sabrina - This is a favorite spot for fall colors.

Beautiful Long Lake in the foreground, gateway to the backcountry and Bishop Pass

ft. all the trail heads are near 9000 ft. so be prepared for the altitude. The trail head to Long Lake is at the South Lake parking lot. It follows the lake on the left hand side. The trail ascends to the left and takes you through a forest.

There are several junctions leading to other lakes. I followed the main trail until I reached Long Lake. It is about 2.5 miles from the trail head and a 1,000 ft. elevation gain. Most of that is established in the last half mile, which consists mainly of switchbacks. Stop frequently, drink plenty of water, enjoy the views and you will make it to Long Lake. The view totally justifies the effort.

Rare red fall colors along Bishop Creek

The town of Bishop

Bishop is named after Samuel A. Bishop, born in Virginia in 1825. He settled in the region with his wife in 1861. She was probably the first white woman in the Owens Valley. Today, the town of Bishop is the largest town of Inyo County. However, it is not the County Seat, **Independence** is.

There are a number of places that are what I call must-sees in town and should not be missed.

Erick Schat's Bakkerij

The first one, surprisingly enough, is a bakery. **Erick Schat's Bakkerij** is one of the main attractions in town. There are days when tourist busses are parked outside and the place is packed with Japanese, European or other people, sampling their products.

What is really important: the bread is great. The Sheepherder bread is their main product. The place doubles up as a Deli so if you want a sandwich to take along on your afternoon hike, this

would be the place. They have been there since 1907. I am the son of a baker, and I can proudly tell you, my father liked their bread too. Bakkerij is the Dutch spelling for bakery, because it is a Dutch bakery.

You will find the **Bakkerij** in the middle of town right on Main Street. On the other side of the street is the Bishop Chamber of Commerce. Check it out for up to date information and some brochures on the area. They do a really good job.

Mountain Light Gallery

When you reach the intersection of Main Street and Line Street (traffic lights) there is another must-see on your left. Turn left on Line Street and take an immediate right to get into the parking lot of the **Mountain Light Gallery.** This is the gallery of the late **Galen Rowell**, mountain climber who turned into world famous photographer.

I had the great pleasure to meet him in person, in 2002, at the Gallery, and shake his hands. I had seen many of his photographs in books, including some of his own, such as **Bay Area Wild**. He was a frequent guest at a TV show broadcast in the Bay Area: **Bay Area**

Old locomotive at Law's Railroad Museum

Back roads. A few months later, after a trip to some remote part of the world, he and his wife Barbara, ironically a pilot, perished outside of Bishop on an early Sunday morning in August, in a charter plane.

This is a very sad story. He climbed mountains. She flew airplanes. The Owens Valley is very wide. They both died in a plane flown by somebody else. I considered him one of the living Ansel Adams'es of the 21th century. Living no more...Learn more about Galen at: *http://www.mountainlight.com*

Another great landscape photographer in town, **Verne Clevenger**, opened a gallery in Bishop, on Main Street, near a Starbuck's. His work is excellent.

Law's Railroad Museum

Another historic place is the Law's Railroad Museum. It is 4.5 miles to the north on US 6. Open year-round until 4pm, except for major holidays, it is an open air museum showing trains, houses, interiors of these houses, etc. Donations are welcome.

Food and Lodging

By now we may have reached the food and lodging department. As far as lodging is concerned, there is no lack of motels in Bishop, unless it is, as I mentioned earlier in the book, Mule Day.

An interesting place to buy food is on the north side of town: the Mahogany Smoked Meats place called **Meadow Farms County Smoke House**. This shop is famous for jerky: beef jerky, elk jerky, etc. Jerky is smoked dried meat. I took a friend there once. She is still ordering jerky from that place via the Internet. So while in Bishop, get some jerky there. They also sell Black Forest Ham, smoked salami and sausages. So when you combine this place and the bakery, you can buy good food for the next couple of days.

By now you may be really hungry. It is a 55 mile drive back to June Lake. How about a stop at Whiskey Creek in Bishop: same beer, same menu as the place in Mammoth, right on Main Street, next to a Bank of America. The layout is different. There is a bar, a restaurant and a nice gift shop.

The other Schat

If you live near Silicon Valley you are probably used to fast Internet connections and a wide range of stores to choose from to purchase accessories for your computer.

The Owens Valley has surprisingly caught up on the Internet part. High speed DSL is available and many hotels are offering WIFI. The predominant ISP appears to Schat.net. I assume it is the grandson of the original baker.

He has a computer store on the main road in downtown Bishop. This is where I looked for and found ink cartridges for one of my printers I took with me on my trip. I was fortunate they carried the correct ink for the printer I had with me.

Opposite: Fall colors along Bishop Creek

LEE VINING TO BRIDGEPORT

We already spent time in Lee Vining in previous chapters in this book. By now you should also know how to get there from June Lake. Get to US 395 and drive north.

The town of Lee Vining was originally called Lakeview until someone discovered that there was another Lakeview in California. There could be no two towns with the same name, yet have a different zip code. That is why the town was renamed and is now called Lee Vining. **Leroy Vining** was one of the first prospectors and settlers in the region.

The first building you see as you enter town is the Lakeview Lodge, on your left, a motel, named after the original name of the town.

Just before the motel building on the right hand side of the road, that holds some additional rooms, you can pick up the Lee Vining Creek trail that we discussed in the Mono Lake chapter.

About five miles north of town, there is a crossroad, both right and left, SR 167. If you go right, you can drive all the way to Hawthorne, NV. This road is called the Pole Line road.

In the late 19th century, there was disbelief that electricity could travel, and if it did, it would have to be in a straight line. We will pick up this story in the Bodie chapter.

Lundy Canyon

If you take a left turn, you will drive through **Lundy Canyon**. This canyon is particularly beautiful in the fall, with all its golden aspen. The canyon was named after **W. J. Lundy** who operated a sawmill supplying Bodie with lumber. There was a lot of mining going on in Lundy Canyon. The Homer mining district was established in 1878 and included the **May Lundy Mine** which is situated at over 9000 ft. overlooking beautiful Crystal Lake.

If you hike high and far enough, you can still find remains of the mining from yesteryear. Lundy's mining lasted longer than most other places as they built a decent transportation system there.

At the end of Lundy Lake is a small resort and store. It is also the beginning of a dirt road that leads to a trail head. Depending on the time of the year it could be easy to drive on, or full of potholes.

Even if you have to walk the extra mile, because you do not want to negotiate driving on that road, the

Opposite: Fantastic view overlooking the Mono Basin from Conway Summit

Beaver ponds in Lundy Canyon

walk to **Lundy Falls** is worth making time for. You can park at the resort or towards the trail head.

Once you are on your way, you will pass beaver ponds Then you will reach a point where you can look at Lundy Falls. Next, the trail turns into switchbacks, and can take you all the way to Helen Lake in the Twenty Lakes Area we discussed in the Tioga Pass chapter.

Of course, that strenuous hike is probably better done in the other direction, as Lundy and Saddlebag are more than 2000 vertical feet apart, Saddlebag being the higher. It is on the top of my wish list of things to do in my lifetime.

Conway Summit

Next on US 395 is the ascent to **Conway Summit**. The road remains wide, fast, yet curves a few times and takes you to an incredible vista point overlooking Mono Lake, the June Lake and Mammoth Lakes area to the south and the White-Inyo Mountain Area

looking southeast. In the fall, there usually is a dramatic display of colorful aspens as you reach the summit.

Virginia Lakes

Less than a mile from this vista point is the turnoff for **Virginia Lakes**. About six miles from US 395 you will find the two Virginia Lakes, probably a lot of fishermen, a parking lot and a trail head.

This is the only hike in this book that qualifies as strenuous, but it is worth every yard, and every breath of air. On my first visit, I just took pictures of Virginia Lakes.

On my second, in June of 2004, I hiked until I could not tell where the trail continued, because of snow. On my third, a month later, I hiked fur-

June 2004 - trail covered with snow

Summit Lake - down below

ce you pass Frog Lakes switchbacks take you to Burro Pass at 11,000 ft.

ther until I thought it was time to turn back. Afterwards I read in a **Hoover Wilderness** brochure about a Sum-mit Lake. It made me believe I had been only half a mile away from a lake at a summit. So in October of the same year I returned and made it all the way to the summit, only to discover that ... Summit Lake was one mile and 900 vertical feet below from where I expected it to be. In the meantime I had achieved a personal high: above 11,000ft. for the first time.

The summit is actually called **Burro Pass** and the view is breathtaking. One day I will get to that lake.

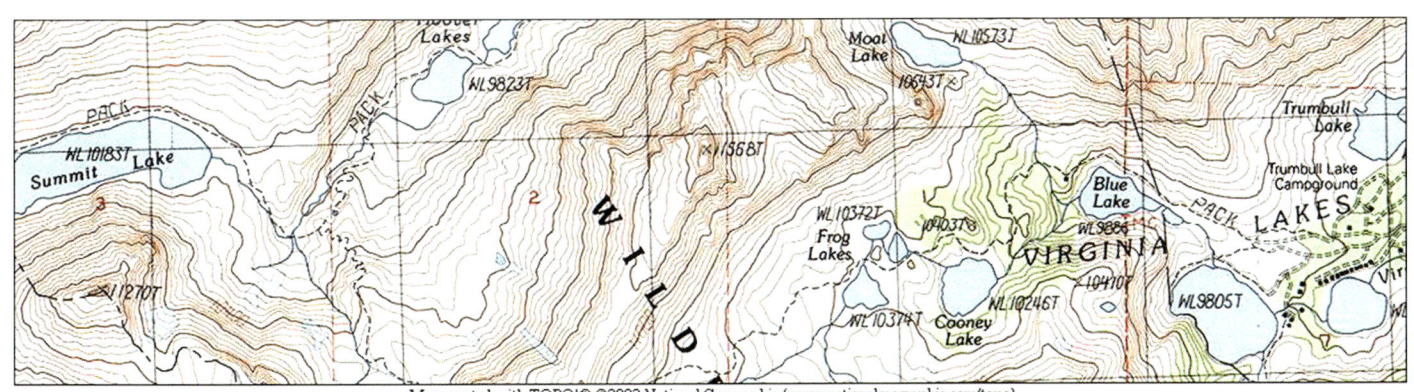

Virginia Lakes Trail to Burro Pass

Map created with TOPO!® ©2003 National Geographic (www.nationalgeographic.com/topo)

Blue Lake - after a tough climb enjoy the view as your reward

Rocks have interesting colors here

You can go all the way to Burro Pass, a 5.5 miles round trip, or just walk as far as you feel like. The trail begins at 9,500 ft. and immediately goes uphill. After a section through a forest you walk over pieces of rock along **Blue Lake**. Above Blue Lake you will meet trees again and the trail turns into switchbacks, giving you some relief from the straight up climb.

Next you will pass **Cooney Lake** and reach **Frog Lakes**. From there it is more of a steady walk until you start

Cooney Lake

the ascent to Burro Pass. I usually suffer the first 20 minutes of a walk; after that it is just a matter of finding the

pace. After all, I have a good excuse, I am a photographer, so I can stop at any time to take another picture.

There are plenty of pictures to be taken on this hike. What makes this canyon particularly interesting is the rock formations you find along the way. Rocks in most canyons are grey in color. Along the trail that begins at Virginia Lakes, they are of a rare burgundy.

So far, the best reference I could find in geology books as a name for this kind of rock, is **Matterhorn**. If you make it all the way up to Burro Pass, you will also see **Matterhorn Peak**, which we will visit again when we get to Twin Lakes.

Bridgeport

Once you get back on US 395 it is about 20 miles to **Bridgeport**. On the way you will notice a sign on the left of the road, remembering **Dog town**. This was another mining town that came and went. Also notice the turnoff to Bodie. We will cover Bodie in a separate chapter.

Bridgeport became the County seat of Mono County when Aurora, the seat of the County before, was attached to Emeralda County of Nevada. All of this happened in 1863. Before then, the place was called Big Meadows.

In 1855 farmers came to Bridgeport Valley and found an abundance of deer, game and fish, and decided to stay.

Bridgeport Court House

Walking on a carpet of aspen leaves

Even today, no matter what time of the year, the meadows along US 395 on the north end of town are remarkably green and moist. There is always cattle grazing, or horses.

The most interesting building in the town of Bridgeport has to be the Court House. Built in 1881, it is the second oldest court house in California. The Court House in San Andreas is the oldest one. We will visit that one in the chapter on SR 4 and Ebbets Pass. The big canon on the front lawn was made in Bodie.

Twin Lakes - Mono Village

Near the end of town, on the left hand side of the road, is a turnoff for **Twin Lakes**. There are several places called Twin Lakes in the Eastern Sierra or elsewhere. We already encountered one in the Mammoth Lakes area. 13 miles from Bridgeport you will reach these Twin Lakes and, at the other end of those lakes, **Mono Village**

Mono Village is mainly a great camp-ground with all the trimmings, a small

The walk through Robinson Canyon is very beautiful in the fall

store, place to rent a boat etc. It is a great recreation spot.

There is a nice hiking opportunity at Mono Village. It is eight miles round trip, but six of those miles are flat, making it a fast walk. It is particularly recommended in the fall, because of all the beautiful aspens.

To get to the trail head, walk through the campground. While still walking through the campground I saw a lot of deer.

Your destination is **Barney Lake**. Once you cross a stream you will first walk through a forest. Next the trail goes

Peaceful Barney Lake: your reward for completing the hike

through a meadow, following Robinson Creek. The scenery is dominated by the Sawtooth Ridge on your left, and its highest mountain, Matterhorn Peak, 12,264 ft.

This hike is at a lower elevation than most others in the book. That should make it easier to those that do not adjust well to the altitude. It starts at just above 7,100 ft. The elevation at Barney Lake is 8,400 ft.

Halfway to the lake a sign indicates that you are entering the Hoover Wilderness. The last mile has a lot of switchbacks with great views. As you climb, look back at the lakes and across the canyon at Matterhorn Peak. Once you reach the lake, relax, have a picnic at the beach and imagine what it was like here 150 years ago. Remember: take only pictures, leave only footprints.

North of Bridgeport

The town of Bridgeport is about the northern border of the area this book is covering, Lone Pine is the southern most town.

However we have taken you through several places and passes to get to this area that are actually north of Bridgeport: **Sonora Pass**, **Monitor Pass** etc.

Should your travels take you back to north of Bridgeport en route to your next destination or even back to the Bay Area, there are a few trips to consider. One is **Lake Tahoe** which can

Matterhorn Peak

be reached by taking Monitor Pass and follow SR 89 all the way to South Lake Tahoe.

Another option is to explore parts of Nevada and drive north on US 395 to **Carson City**, visit its state museum and make a side trip to **Genoa** or **Virginia City,** a mining town made famous by the TV series Bonanza.

BISHOP TO LONE PINE

This is the longest day trip suggested in this book. Of course, you can combine visiting the places covered in this chapter with those in the Mammoth to Bishop chapter. Also, if you drive to June Lake from Los Angeles, you may want to visit some of these spots on your way over to June Lake or back to L.A. and spend a night in **Lone Pine** to do so.

From June Lake, get to the by now very familiar June Lake junction and drive south. About 15 miles past Bishop, you will reach **Big Pine**.

Ancient Bristlecone Pines

Right before the town of Big Pine, turn left on SR 168. After about a mile or so, you will cross the Owens River. On your right, there is a road with an interesting sign: " *Pavement ends in 25 miles*". This is one of the alternate roads into Death Valley, if you have the right vehicle for it. It will take you through **Last Chance Canyon** and goes by the **Eureka Dunes.**

Obviously we do not have the right vehicle. 13 miles from US 395 you reach **Westgard Pass**, renamed after A.I.Westgard who headed a caravan for the Indiana Automobile Manufacturers Association. Prior it was the **Deep Springs Valley Toll Road**. Near Westgard Pass the road is one lane only, so drive slowly.

SR 168 is an interesting alternate route to get from the Eastern Sierra to Las Vegas. It eventually connects with US 95. Our destination, **Schulman Grove**, requires a left turn, however, onto White Mountain Road. It is another ten miles to its Visitor Center.

As you gain elevation, for those not at the wheel, great views of the Sierra Crest open up, looking west. About a mile before Schulman Grove there is a must-stop, must-see vista point and trail. It is called and marked as **The Sierra View Overlook**.

Park and take the short walk. You are 6,700 ft. above the Owens Valley and have the greatest of views looking at the entire crest of the Sierra Nevada Mountain Range, from south of Mt. Whitney all the way to Tioga Pass. Bring your camera! There is a display showing the names of all the peaks you are gazing at.

As you reach Schulman Grove, the paved road is about to end, You have also reached an elevation of 10,000 ft., so take it easy. A dirt road continues for another 12 miles into the White

Opposite: Bristlecone Pine trees along the Discovery trail

Sierra Crest as seen from Sierra View Overlook

Mountains to another grove of trees, called the **Patriarch Grove**, 11,200ft. I have never made an attempt as I prefer to stay on paved roads.

Bristlecone pine trees happen to be the oldest living trees on the planet. They are not very tall and appear more dead than alive, but some of them are almost 5,000 years old. They grow in a very barren terrain with a lot of bad weather. Bristlecone Pine trees can be found in six southern states in America, but the ones in the White Mountains are the oldest.

Schulman Grove is named after Dr. Edmund Schulman (1908-1958) who was a dendrochronologist at the University of Arizona. **Dendrochronology** is the science of using tree rings as a measurement of time.

His findings revealed how old these trees actually are and created a lot of attention, in particular his article in National Geographic. Unfortunately, he passed away too soon.

A very nice Visitor Center welcomes you. At 10,000 ft. this is possibly the highest Visitor Center in California.

Check the displays inside, talk to the Park Ranger and in any case get a copy of the book about the Park as well as the $1.00 guide describing the walk. Weather permitting, Schulman Grove should be open from Memorial Day until early November. Check with Caltrans before you start your day trip.

There are two walks at Schulman Grove One is called the **Discovery Trail**. It starts at the other side of the parking lot and is only a mile long. I recommend the other one, which is called the **Methuselah** walk.

...istlecone Pine tree along the Discovery Trail

Eastern California Museum

A few blocks away from the main road, on Grant street, is the **Eastern California museum**. It is full of artifacts from the mining days as well as interesting displays about **Manzanar**. Outside there is an open air museum with old buildings and all kinds of mining equipment.

One could spend a full day exploring what is on display inside the museum. Of particular interest are the original skis and other gear of famous mountaineer **Norman Clyde**. He made many first ascents in the High Sierra. He also wrote a book: "**Close-up of the High Sierra**". It is excellent and a rare find, as it was out of print for a while. I picked up a copy of a new edition at the bookstore inside the mu-

Dr. Schulman named the oldest tree he found the **Methusaleh** tree. For its own protection the tree is not marked. This walk is about four miles and the trail starts at the Visitor Center. When it forks, swing right. Remember that you are at an altitude of 10,000 ft. so take it slowly. There are some great views along the way.

Independence

South of Big Pine is the town of **Independence**, formerly known as Little Pine. The town has become the county seat of Inyo county in 1866. There are some interesting things to see in town.

County Courthouse

First and foremost there is the Inyo County Courthouse. It was built four times, as it was destroyed by fire and then again by the 1872 earthquake. It was built for a third time in 1887. The present building is from 1926. Each time I see the building, it makes me think of the White House.

County Courthouse, Independence

Obelisk at cemetary, Manzanar National Historic Site

seum. My favorite part of the museum are the displays of old newspapers and signs from about a hundred years ago.

Some of them are very entertaining, for example: "**If I am not on the job, you can find me at the aqueduct**", or "**Steal my horse, run off with my wife but damn you, don't touch my water!**" All were familiar quotes in the Owens Valley during the aqueduct days.

Mary Austin House

Back on the main road is the **Mary Austin** (1868 - 1934) house. Mary Austin was best known for her book **The Land of Little Rain.** The house is not open to the public.

If eating or drinking is what you have in mind, Independence is not the place. You will have to go to Lone Pine.

Manzanar National Historic Site

In the course of its brief history, this site has been many things. It was the site where the Owens Valley Paiute Indians lived. Later it became farm-land, apple farms in particular. That explains the name. Manzana is Spanish for apple.

In more recent years, Manzanar has become famous because of yet another unfortunate Owens Valley story.

In 1942, the United States government ordered more than 110,000 Japanese men, women, and children to leave their homes and detained them in remote, military-style camps. Manzanar War Relocation Center was one of ten camps where Japanese American citizens and resident Japanese aliens were interned during World War II.

I worked with a lady who's parents spent several years in Manzanar. I never dared asking her what that experience must have been like.

Manazanar is located between Independence and Lone Pine. You can visit it year round. There is an Interpretive Center. You can also take a 3.2 mile self-guided car tour. Do not expect to see much, as none of the original buildings are still standing, except for the guard posts near the entrance.

On the west side of the grounds is the cemetery, with an obelisk in the center of it. But there always is the dramatic backdrop of the Sierra Crest right in front of you. Ansel Adams took pictures there, including his **Mount Williamson from Manzanar**.

Inside the Interpretive Center you can find a lot of information on what it was like living there during WW II. Of course, there is also a gift shop.

Throughout the Center you find TV monitors where you can see a recording of the official pardon signed by President Reagan in 1988. On that day, the US government officially admitted that a mistake had been made way back then and awarded all survivors with a sum of money.

A note of irony: Manzanar interned over 10,000 people behind barbed wire with no due process of law. Some internees found it ironic that the nearest town, six miles to the north, is named **Independence.**

Lone Pine

Interagency Visitor Center

More than 100 miles south of June Lake is the town of Lone Pine. Start your visit by driving to the southern tip of town. This is where the Inter-

Mount Whitney and the Alabama Hills from Lone Pine

agency Visitor Center is. It is located at the intersection of US 395 and SR 136.

This is a very unique location. SR 136 is the road that takes you 100 miles into Death Valley, the lowest point, 282 ft. below sea level. From the Visitor Center you have a great view, looking west, of Mount Whitney, the highest mountain, 14,495 ft. The lowest point and highest point within 100 miles: only in California !

History of Mt. Whitney

In 1864, there was a geological survey performed to investigate all the high peaks in the Sierra. The tallest peak was named after the chief of the survey, Josiah D. Whitney. For years, there was confusion about which mountain actually was Mount Whitney. In 1871, Clarence King climbed what he believed to be the highest mountain (now Mount Langley), so

Rock formation in the Alabama Hills - I feel it looks like a giant mammoth

he ended up on the wrong Mount Whitney! Several people have actually climbed the true highest peak, including some fishermen. That is why for years what is now Mount Whitney was called **Fisherman's Peak**. Mr. King made up for his mistake and climbed the correct Mount Whitney a few years later.

Food and Lodging

There are several nice motels in town. I usually stay in the **Best Western Frontier** - out of habit more than anything else. It is very reasonably priced and has a swimming pool, which is great in the summer time.

There are also many places to eat in town. The folks in the motel recom-

mended **Seasons** and T**he Merry-go-round**. On a recent trip I discovered a Mexican restaurant called **Bonanza**. Their **Chili Colorado** was to die for. For the thirsty among you there is **Jake's Saloon**. They have Mojave Red on tap, a beer brewed in the desert by the Mojave Brewing Company.

The saloon is also a Clamper Watering Hole (Slim Princess Chapter 395).

Some nights they have gunfights where locals dressed up in costumes from the Gold Rush days shoot at each other across the pool table. An hour later you can watch it on video. After all, this is Lone Pine, site of many westerns. On more quiet days you can simply join their pool contest.

Alabama Hills.

If you look towards Mount Whiitney from the Visitor Center you will notice an abundance of large brown rocks in the foreground. These are the Alabama Hills. There is a famous Ansel Adams photograph, ***"Mount Whitney and the Alabama Hills from Lone Pine"*** It may have been taken from the very spot where you are standing.

During the Civil War, these hills were named after a Confederate Cruiser by the same name. So it is not the state of Alabama that these interesting rocks are named after.

To get closer to the Alabama Hills from the Visitor Center, drive north to the center of town and turn left at the traffic light, the only one in town, onto ***Whitney Portal Road***.

Alabama Hills, White Mountains and Owens Lake from Horseshoe Meadow Road

Horseshoe Meadows

This side trip is highly recommended in late afternoon, as that time of day offers the best light. After a mile or so on Whitney Portal Road, take the left turn marked ***Horseshoe Meadows***. A windy, but very well maintained paved road takes you to above 10,000 ft. elevation. The road itself is 20 miles each way, but it is worth every yard for its spectacular views.

Stop many times where it is safe to do so. You will look over the entire Owens Valley. The Alabama Hills structure is on your left, the White Mountains right across and more to the right Owens Lake. That lake, of course, is now a dry lake. Imagine what this place would have looked like more than one hundred years ago, when both the river and the lake had plenty of water in them, and were a natural source of irrigation for all the green pastures surrounding them - including ***Manzanar*** with its apple orchards.

Nevertheless, today's view is also spectacular in its own right. If you follow the road to the very end you will see a radical change of the nature surrounding you.

Alabama Hills along Movie Road

Movie Road is on the right hand side of Whitney Portal Road, about a mile from town. It is a wide sandy road, that is very passable. Notice the white rock with the commemorative plaque on it, right on the corner. This is another example of the good work of the Clamper organization, mentioned elsewhere in this book.

Just drive around or, better still, walk around and admire all the interesting rocks and compare them with the movie locations on the map.

The next time you watch a western movie, the experience will be like never before, as you will be looking for those spots you have visited.

You have left the dry desert environment and now drive through a pine forest until you reach the parking lot at the very end. There you find trail heads to many backpacking trips across the Sierra mountain range, all the way into Kings Canyon National Park.

This is not doable as a day hike. It is just interesting to know that reaching Kings Canyon or Sequoia National Park from the Eastern Sierra, which would require a major detour by car, can be done on foot.

Movie Road

The **Alabama Hills** have been used a lot by Hollywood. Many movies were filmed here. Examples are **"Gunga Din"**, **"How the West Was Won"**, the TV series **"Rawhide"** and a long scene in one of the **Star Trek** movies. Since 1990, Lone Pine even has its own film festival in October.

At the Visitor Center you can buy a video or book showing where exactly John Wayne came around the corner, Gary Grant showed up in Gunga Din etc. Or ask for the free one page map.

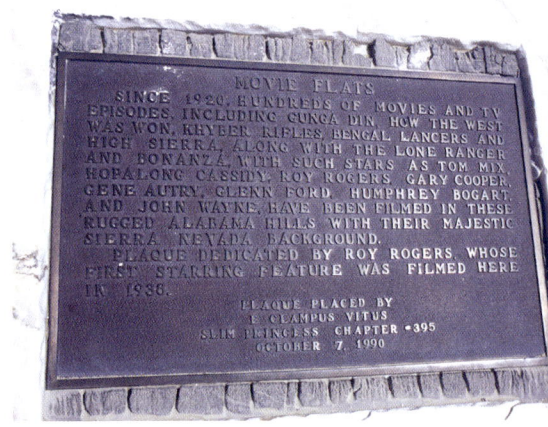

Movie Flats plaque dediicated by the Clampers

vie Museum in downtown lone Pine

is in very thin air to reach an elevation of close to 15,000 ft. Surprisingly enough this trail is very popular, a comparison with a freeway is not too far fetched, and reservations need to be made to do the climb.

Check the Visitor Center in Lone Pine for more information. There you can also buy a book explaining how to prepare for the ascent, suggestions on what to wear, what to bring, and where to spend the night on the way up. If you are thinking about taking on this adventure, take a copy home and study it by next year.

As you let your imagination go, you will recognize all kinds of structures, animals, demons etc. in the shapes of the rock. One structure I looked at, to me at least, appears like a dead mammoth. Judge for yourself, I have included it in the book.

No trip to the Alabama Hills and Movie Road would be complete without a visit to the **Movie Museum**. It is located in Lone Pine, on the west side of US 395. Inside you find posters, costumes, books and all kinds of information on the movies that were made in or around Lone Pine.

Whitney Portal

If you continue on Whitney Portal Road, with superb views looking back at the Owens Vallley, you will reach **Whitney Portal**. It is a perfect place for a picnic, and has tables and chairs for it. The higher elevation, about 10,000 ft., the shades of the trees and a nearby waterfall, bring you great relief from the desert heat down below.

Whitney Portal also happens to be the trail head for those brave people that climb Mount Whitney. From that spot it is 11 miles, one way. However, this

South of Lone Pine

There are several interesting spots south of Lone Pine, but quite a few miles away. So if you reached Lone Pine as part of a day trip from June Lake, now is the time to turn back.

If, however, you are spending the night in Lone Pine or are driving to or from Los Angeles, you may want to take the extra time to stop along some of these places, located between Lone Pine and Mojave.

Olancha

About 20 miles south of Lone Pine is the small town of **Olancha**. There is an intersection with SR 190 and a sign indicating 100 miles to Death Valley. The turnoff in Lone Pine takes you along the east side of Owens Lake but joins this same road near the remains of the old mining town **Keeler**.

Indian Wells

About 75 miles south of Lone Pine, US 395 will turn southeast at the junction of SR 14. If you continue on SR 14 towards Mojave, you will see on your left the towns of **Inyokern** and **Ridgecrest.**

The name Inyokern is easy to explain, as you find yourself at the border of the counties of Inyo and Kern**.** Ridgecrest is the larger of the two towns and offers an alternate route to Death Valley, via **Trona.**

On the west side of US 395 is the home the **Mojave Brewing Company**, mentioned elsewhere in this book. The beer is made using water from a small spring, next to the building. **Indian Wells.**

Red Rock Canyon State Park

This is also the name of the valley you are driving through. The brewery also hosts a popular restaurant. Limo services from Ridgecrest are used by people that like to dine there.

Red Rock Canyon State Park

Only 24 miles north of the town of Mojave (100 miles south of Lone Pine) is **Red Rock Canyon State Park.** Located in the middle of the Mojave desert, this park offers several interesting rock formations. They remind me of the red rocks in Bryce Canyon National Park in Utah.

The park has a Visitor Center and a campground. Expect it to be very hot and bring plenty of water, no matter how short a trip you are planning. There are a few very interesting, short, nature trails in the park.. As you go for a walk through the park, notice all the Joshua trees with their diverse shapes.

Opposite: Rocks in Alabama Hills and Sierra crest

XI

BODIE STATE PARK

The town of **Bodie** lies at 8369 ft. and is about a 45 minute drive from June Lake. Bodie was named after **Waterman S. Body,** a Dutchman from Poughkeepsie, NY, who discovered gold there in 1859. He never really saw the development of the town named after him, as he died in that same year in a snowstorm. By 1879 the town had a population of 10,000 and was considered one of the richest mining towns of the west.

A lot of the buildings in town were destroyed in a fire in 1932, started by as little boy nicknamed "**Bodie Bill**". 175 buildings are still standing, representing about 5% of what was there when the town was booming.

By 1937 the population of the town was down to a single digit number. In 1962, Bodie became a State Park. The buildings were never restored but kept in a state of "**arrested decay**". The only efforts done is to make sure to prevent them from further deterioration, but not to restore them in their original state.

The best time to visit is, like most of the Eastern Sierra, late spring to early fall. The other half of the year, Bodie competes with Truckee for the coldest spot in the entire state of California. The temperature there can be as low as -20 ° F. There is almost no vegetation in Bodie to protect you from the wind. That, and the altitude, explains the cold temperatures.

Turn left at the June Lake junction and drive through Lee Vining to Conway Summit. About halfway to Bridgeport is the turnoff for SR 270 to Bodie. The first 10 miles of this 13 mile road are paved. The last three miles are not: it is a well maintained dirt road.

Pay the entrance fee and also buy the brochure for the self guided tour. Inquire at what time the Park is closing that day. As you find your way to the parking lot notice the cemetery on your left, just outside of town. Carry water, a camera and, if you have one, a polarizing filter.

Your tour will begin on **Green Street**. One of the first buildings on your left is the Methodist Church from 1882. The last service there was in 1932.

The brochure explains the background and history of most buildings, even the ones that are no longer there.

Take your time, walk around and take pictures. The best time to do that is early morning or late afternoon. Then you have the best light conditions. In the summer time the Park closes at 7 PM, 4 PM the rest of the year. This

Swazey Hotel. One would assume that 100 years ago the building did not look like all it wanted was to fall down

Boone, a direct descendent of Daniel Boone. The store window looks exactly like it did before the store permanently closed, probably in 1937, but it gives the impression that the last time the store was open was yesterday.

Next to the store is the old gas station and, usually, and old car. If you do not see the car, look for it during your walk around town. They sometimes take it for a ride.

Across the street is the **Wheaton and Hollis hotel**, as well as the public rest rooms. Look through the window and notice the pool table. The schoolhouse up Green Street is also very interesting, as you can take a look at the old classroom.

Boone Store and Warehouse. It looks like it never closed.

Dinner table, probably set in 1936

typically means you cannot catch a sunset in Bodie.

The purpose of the remainder of this chapter is not to try to walk you by all the buildings, but only to mention

a few where you absolutely have to make a stop.

On the corner of Green and Main Street is the **Boone Store and Warehouse** (1879), owned by Harvey

...gan inside the church

Note that with most buildings this is all you can do in Bodie: look inside through the window. They cannot be entered by visitors.

Occasionally, by appointment only, photographers are allowed inside some of th buildings. That explains some of the photographs you find in the calendars or the **Photographing Bodie** book they sell there. I so far never had the pleasure of doing this.

My favorite building is on the other corner of Main and Green Street: the **Swazey Hotel**. It looks like it has been trying to fall down for years but never did. This is arrested decay at its best. It is also hard to imagine that a building this small contained a hotel and a store.

I was looking for a spot to load a roll of film and found this old sleigh

Old car in Bodie. Some days they drive it around   -   Opposite page: Old wagon wheel

On the other side of the street is the museum, open from Memorial Day to Labor Day. Built in 1877, it functioned as the Miners Union Hall. Victor Cain converted it into a museum in 1943.

Today it is also a Visitor Center and a gift shop. There are no restaurants in Bodie, unlike 130 years ago. So when you drive back to June Lake, you may with want to stop in Lee Vining.

Note, as you leave Bodie , that there is another dirt road more to the left. This road will eventually join the **Pole Line Road** that comes from Hawthorne, NV. Do not attempt to take this road.

XII

THE GOLD COUNTRY, SR 4 AND EBBETS PASS

As mentioned in Chapter Two, the most beautiful pass to cross the Sierra Nevada is **Ebbets Pass**. It opens later and closes sooner than most others, so always check road conditions first. As it takes you through some of the most interesting places of the Gold Country I recommend spending at least one extra day there before continuing on to the Eastern Sierra.

Another option is to visit most of what is described in this chapter when you return from the Eastern Sierra and visit Yosemite Valley. The places within **Calaveras County** listed here can easily be visited in a single day and you would want a place to stay somewhere west of Yosemite Valley anyhow.

Murphys is a great place to spend at least one night. It is only 8 miles east of **Angels Camp** and has a lot to offer. There is wine tasting in town, historic

buildings, including the Murphys Hotel, and it is short distance to the **Big Trees State Park**. It also has a slightly higher elevation than Angels Camp, making it less hot in the summer.

In earlier days, State Route 4 from Angels Camp to Ebbets Pass was called the **Big Tree Route**. Today it is called Ebbets Pass. In 2005, the road was honored with the status of National Scenic Byway. Only seven roads in California are designated Scenic Byways.

One of them is, not surprisingly, the Tioga Road. The roads along Big Sur and SR 190 through Death Valley are two other examples.

The road was originally travelled by Miwok, Mokelumne and Washoe Indians. Today, it takes you 58 miles from Angels Camp through Calaveras

and Alpine counties to where the road ends, at the junction with SR 89, Monitor Pass.

Expect this road to become busier in the years to come as a lot of new development is planned at the Bear Valley ski resort. Hopefully this will have little effect in the summertime.

To get there from the Bay Area follow the same initial itinerary listed in Chapter 2 to HWY 5 north. Stay on it until you reach Stockton. In Stockton, take the 4 East exit. This is a crosstown freeway, very fast, connecting HWY 5 with HWY 99. Take 99 south for about one mile and then exit to get on SR 4 East. This will take you to Angels Camp , the biggest town in Calaveras County.

You will drive through **Copperopolis**, a living proof that not all mining done

Mosquito Lakes, just west of Pacific Grade, the other pass on this road

in the Gold Country was for gold. It is about 45 miles from Stockton to Angels Camp. Once you reach SR 49 in Angels Camp, turn right. After a few miles through town, turn left where SR 49 and SR 4 split again to reach Murphys.

Murphys

Murphys is known as the **Queen of the Sierra** and has an elevation of 2,171ft. The town was named after John and Daniel Murphy, who came to California, like so many others, to seek gold. They arrived in what is now Murphys in 1848.

Historic Murphys Hotel

Today it is basically not much more than a one street town with the Murphys Historic Hotel as one of its main attractions. The hotel is an interesting

place to spend a night or two. The original was built in 1856 but was destroyed by fire three years later. It was immediately rebuilt. It used to be called the **Sperry and Perry Hotel** and now it is simply the Murphys Historic Hotel.

When I stayed there room rates were around $100 a night. The Saloon and the rooms of the main building are part of the original 1859 structure.

If you arrive in Murphys before 4 PM you can park the car, check into the hotel and then go for a walk. Both Calaveras and Amador Counties are actually wine country. Down Main Street, there are several places to go wine tasting. **Zinfandel** wines are my favorite. I found a great one at **Millaire**, just down the street, but this is only one of many. There are also a lot of antique shops.

After dark it is of course time for dinner, which you can have at the historic dining room, or, in the summer, in the garden, at the Murphys Hotel or check out some of the other restaurants in town.

After dinner it is probably time to go back to your room and plan the next day. I am assuming you want to spend

a day travelling around in the Gold Country and only move on to June Lake the next day. I enjoyed it when I did it this way: very relaxing.

Angels Camp

Angels Camp is named after Henry Angel, from Rhode Island. He opened a trading post in 1848 at the place that is now named after him. It is the largest town of Calaveras County, but

still small. It became famous when Mark Twain wrote his short story: **The Jumping Frog of Calaveras County.**

As a result you can now find a statue of Mark Twain in the park, a statue of a frog near the intersection of SR 49 and SR 4 east, an annual frog jumping competition, in May, and a lot of frog

T-shirts. That is not all, just like Hollywood has its Walk of Fame, Angels Camp has its own. On Main Street you find metal plaques on the pavements, picturing frogs, their names, the year they won the leaping frog contest as well as the distance they jumped.

Historic Main Street has some buildings dating back to the Gold Rush days and the town is a good alternative for lodging if you cannot find any accommodation in Murphys. Pick up a free brochure at the Visitor Center on Main Street. It shows all the buildings and a little bit of their history.

San Andreas

This is not where the **San Andreas** fault is. A few miles north of Angels Camp is the town of San Andreas, the county seat of Calaveras County. One of the side streets of SR 49 is old

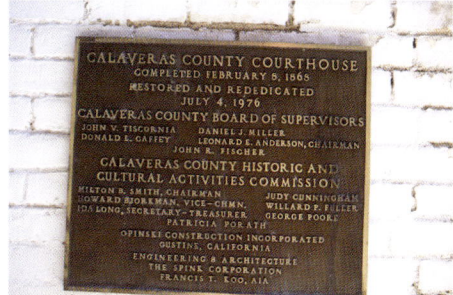
Sign at Calaveras County Courthouse

Main Street and there you will find the interesting **Calaveras County Museum and Archives**. It is located in the building of the old Courthouse, the oldest in the state. When a friendly volunteer worker showed me around the museum she told me I could not see the courtroom as there was actually a court in session, because of some overflow problem in town.

A little later she did let me in and I saw a judge making notes. A picture of **Abraham Lincoln** was hanging against the wall right behind him. Just close your eyes and picture you are in the 1860's. She also showed me the jail where **Black Bart** stayed. This man was sentenced in the same courthouse in the 1880's. He had robbed many stage coaches, reportedly without even carrying a weapon. A laundry tag from a place in San Francisco, showing his real name, eventually resulted in his capture. Black Bart is part of Gold Country history. There is even a restaurant named after him.

Mokelumne Hill

The name means people from Mokel. A little off SR 49 is this relic of the Gold Country days. It had a population of 15,000 at one point and was

San Andreas Courthouse

the County Seat of Calaveras County for about 10 years. It has many interesting buildings, including the **Hotel Leger** and some old artifacts that photographers will cherish. If you have an extra half hour or so, make the little detour.

I noticed a very old car in the town of Mokulemne Hill

Hotel Leger

Jackson

Jackson is the County seat of Amador County and is located near the intersection of SR 49 and SR 88, one of the alternate routes we discussed. North of town are the famous Kennedy Mine and Kennedy Wheels Park. The old main street has some old buildings dating back to the Gold Rush days.

Sutter Creek

Sutter Creek is named after the same John Sutter who created Sutter Mill in Coloma, north of Placerville. This is where the first gold was discovered which marked the beginning of the Gold Rush. John Sutter was born in Germany from Swiss parents, so some people may want to pronounce his name differently. Ironically, Mr. Sutter was broke when he died. Sutter Creek is a very nice town with many old buildings along its Main Street.

Volcano

There are many more towns north on SR 49 but every extra mile driven is an extra mile that needs to be driven back so it is probably time to go back to Murphys.

One side trip to consider on the way back to Murphys is **Volcano**. You can reach it from Sutter Creek. There is a turnoff in the middle of town, on the east side of SR 49. You can work your way back to a junction on SR 88, just north of Jackson. This is an opportunity to do some driving around in the Gold Country, off the beaten path.

Volcano is a very picturesque town in the **Mother Lode**, as the Gold Country is often called. To me it appears more like an open air museum. It has a large collection of well preserved buildings. There is a school, a brewery, the George Hotel, the Masonic Hall etc.

Back to Murphys

In this part we cover the places along SR 4 east of Murphys, all the way to Ebbets Pass. You can visit some of them in reverse order and return to Murphys. This is recommended if you want to include the Snowshoe

Brewing Company. Or you can make a few stops along the way when you drive from Murphys to June Lake via Ebbets Pass. It is about a 3 1/2 hour drive from Murphys to June Lake, not including the various stops you might make.

Arnold

Just a few miles east of Murphys is the town of Arnold. (4000 ft.) It is a good stop on the way to the Calaveras State Park of Big Trees. It is also a good idea to fill the tank there as there will be very few gas stations from there on, if any.

Arnold is also the home of the **Snowshoe Brewing Company**. They serve and sell excellent ales that are brewed on the premises.

You can get the beers in other places as well, but this is an opportunity to check out the source and maybe have a chat with the brewer. The beers have some interesting names, such as **Thompson Pale Ale, Extra Special Blizzard, Grizzly Brown Ale and Snoweizen Wheat**. There is a story behind this.

e Big Stump

Snowshoe Thompson

The first part of the story is that his real name was not even Thomson. He was born in 1827 as John A Tostenson in Telemark in Norway. The next part is that nobody seems to agree about the spelling of his new name: is it Thompson or Thomson?

What really matters though are the accomplishments of this man. From 1856 to 1876 he worked for the US Postal Service. By itself this appears nothing special. However, Thompson carried the mail, on his back, from Murphys to Carson City, over the Sierra Mountain range.

He sometimes carried 60 pounds on his back. To cover this distance of 90 miles he used snowshoes he made himself, remembering how to do it from his days in Norway, Hence the name **Snowshoe Thompson**.

Calaveras Big Trees State Park

The main attraction along SR 4 on your way to Ebbets Pass is, without a doubt, this beautiful state park. Make sure you include a visit in your plans and schedule.

In our tidbits of history we mentioned some names of people who must have been the first white men to have seen these trees. The person who gets the credit for making the trees famous was a hunter, Augustus Dowd, who discovered the trees in 1852, while chasing a wounded grizzly bear. He went back to Murphys and told his story. Soon people started to visit what became known as the Calaveras North Grove.

A year later some entrepreneurs decided to strip the very same tree, now called the **Discovery tree**, of its bark. They felled it and took it on a travelling exhibit. It took 5 men 22 days to do so. The tree was the largest tree in the North Grove, over 25 feet in diameter at the base, and 300 feet tall.

When the tree rings were counted it was estimated to be 1244 years old. What is left of the tree is now called **The Big Stump**. It is often used at the beginning of guided tours and as it is so large the guide and the entire group can stand on it.

Giant Sequoias may not be the oldest trees, **Bristlecone Pines** are, nor the tallest trees, **Coastal Redwoods** are, but they are the biggest trees. The North Grove became a California Park in 1931.

There is an entrance fee at the Park. Sometimes it is self registration, so make sure you carry cash. There is a very nice Visitor Center with a small museum showing displays of the local fauna and flora as well as a great gift shop. They also sell the self-guided tours there for both the North Grove and South Grove trails.

The North Grove trail is only one mile long, walking distance from the Visitor Center and wheel chair accessible. No hiking booths are required. You walk on a wooden pavement almost the entire way.

The South Grove is about a three an a half mile walk, but very easy. It is about a nine mile drive on a paved

road to get to the South Grove Campground and trail head.

Dorrington

I found out about this gem from a friend. Two miles east of the park is the small town of **Dorrington** (4,730 ft.). There is a historic hotel, which has been there since 1860, and next door is a Saloon. It is called the **Lube Room**.

They make the best burgers I have ever eaten. My favorite kind is called a **spicy lube**. They also serve the Snowshoe Extra Special Blizzard ale. All the ornaments on the ceiling and against the walls (another **ECV** watering hole) and the nutshells on the floor give the place a special charm.

After a nice walk around the South Grove or North Grove you probably have come up with an appetite, and in all likelihood still a long drive ahead of you. This is the place to take care of that.

Ebbets Pass

Once you leave Dorrington the road reaches higher elevations and crosses the Calaveras/Alpine County Line at

Bear Valley (7.073 ft.) You now enter what is called the **California Alps**. After another three miles you will pass beautiful **Lake Alpine**.

This is where the road narrows to what is basically a one and a half lane road with no center line. Take it slow as there are also many sharp blind curves.

If motorists stay on the right hand side of the road, usually it is no problem for cars to be able to cross on this road. The views are spectacular. You will cross two summits. Right before the first one, **Pacific Grade**, 8050 ft., you pass Mosquito Lakes. **Ebbets Pass** itself is 8,730 ft.

In between those two summits I had a not so pleasant reminder that this is **Alpine County.** I was driving back home on a sunny Sunday in October and had just crossed Ebbets Pass, in the convertible car, when I heard cowbells. This reminded me of the Alps, I remember from my youth: Switzerland.

Next I saw a few folks on horseback and some dogs, immediately followed by many big cows coming down from the mountain. Before I knew it I was surrounded by cows: in front of me, behind me, to my left, to my right. I could not stop nor could I pass them.

This lasted for a few miles until the people finally found a way to stop them and let me pass. I am telling you, if the head of a cow is right next to yours, only a foot away:, it is **big**.

To this day people have been asking me why I did not take a picture (The answer: I had both hands on the steering wheel).

Thirteen miles past Ebbets Pass you will reach the junction with SR 89. Take a left to go over Monitor Pass, not really a pass in comparison. After 18 miles and great views overlooking Carson Valley you will reach US 395, just south of the Nevada border, by Topaz.

Until a few years ago, the **Monitor Pass** drive was very beautiful in the fall but in 2007 there was a big fire that burned most of the aspens.

It is another 70 miles to June Lake. You drive through the small towns of **Coleville** and **Walker**, pass the Sonora Pass junction and reach Bridgeport.

Drive through the town of Lee Vining, and follow US 395 until you reach the South June Lake Junction. Fill the tank at the gas station there, if needed, and turn right.

You pass June Lake, the lake, and then enter June Lake, the town. Welcome to paradise !

XIII

YOSEMITE VALLEY

Visiting **Yosemite Valley** from June Lake and driving all the way back in one day is pushing the limit of the 200 mile a day rule. However, if this is your only opportunity to visit beautiful Yosemite Valley, go for it.

Not visiting this wonderful place is not an option at all. An easier way to visit would be if you have organized your vacation in such a way that you plan to stay in places nearby Yosemite Valley, such as Oakhurst, Mariposa or Coulterville after driving back from the Eastern Sierra.

These three towns are good stepping stones towards wherever your next destination may be, probably **San Francisco** or **Los Angeles**. It also gives you an opportunity to visit the Gold Country, as discussed in the previous chapters, because this is exactly where these towns are located.

Opposite: Great look at Half Dome from Glacier Point

There are many guides on Yosemite National Park, including the ultimate one written by the late Stephen Medley. I merely list the places that I feel should be stopped at, looked at, and photographed, if a single drive through the valley is the only option your schedule permits. I do recommend however to purchase a good guide on Yosemite National Park if you want to spend time in the park itself.

History in a nutshell

The first white people to have ever set foot in Yosemite Valley were probably the members of the Mariposa Battalion, searching for Indians on March 27, 1851. They were sent there to deal with all the conflicts between miners and Indians after gold was discovered in 1849. Later, on October 1, 1890, Yosemite National Park was created.

Roads into Yosemite Valley

Today, there are three main roads leading into Yosemite Valley. One we are already familiar with: SR 120, or the Tioga Road. The two other roads are SR 140 from Mariposa and SR 41 from Oakhurst.

Yosemite Valley is about 75 miles from Tioga Pass. Once you reach the junction at **Crane Flat**, turn left to reach Yosemite Valley, another 16 miles. There are no gas stations in the valley so you may want to fill up at the Crane Flat station.

Since the early 1970s, one-way traffic patterns exist in the valley. So once you enter you will start on your right.

At the intersection with SR 41, also turn right, you can visit the rest of the Valley later. This road will take you to what I consider to be the numero uno spot in Yosemite Valley. After a few miles you are about to enter a tunnel: don't.

Tunnel View

Instead, park at the parking lot right before the tunnel. There is **Tunnel View**, also called **Inspiration Point**. This is what to most people has been the first ever view of Yosemite: breathtaking. You see **El Capitan**, **Half Dome**, **Bridalveil Fall** and a lot of tourists.

Glacier Point

If the Glacier Point Road is open, drive through the tunnel and follow SR 41 until you hit the left turnoff for Glacier Point. It is about 30 miles from Yosemite Valley to Glacier Point. At Glacier Point you will find yourself way above the Valley, almost at the same level as Half Dome and facing spectacular views.

I have seen many people there looking through binoculars watching folks climbing Half Dome, appearing to be the size of an ant. **John Muir** and **President Roosevelt** sat on a rock there and now a lot of people want to

Half Dome from Sentinel Bridge

do the same. Don't as you could fall down and kill yourself.

Mariposa Grove

If you drive back down from Glacier Point you can either turn left on SR 41

nel View - For a lot of people their first view of Yosemite Valley.

or right to go back to Yosemite Valley. The left turn will take you to the **Mariposa Grove of Sequoia Trees**, at the outskirts of the Park.

If you have the time to visit, do it. 14 miles beyond the Park Entrance is the town of Oakhurst, a nice place to stay before moving on. I stayed at the Best

Western there a few times. It turned out that the original owner is Belgian.

Bridalveil Fall

Once you return to the Park, passing Tunnel Vew and reaching the Valley again, the next stop is **Bridalveil Fall**. This is where SR 41 meets the valley

road. Park the car, walk and get wet, as you get closer to the fall itself. Bridalveil Fall is 620 feet tall.

Sentinel Bridge.

From there get back on the one-way road and see if there is parking across Sentinel Bridge. From that bridge

Upper Yosemite Falls as seen from near Sentinel Bridge

you have the best view of Half Dome. From the parking lot, walk into the adjacent meadow. This is a great spot to look at Upper and Lower **Yosemite Falls**.

Get back in the car and try your chances to find a parking spot in the center of the Valley, so you can check out the Visitor Center and the **Ansel Adams Gallery.**

Valley View

There is one more stop to be made before leaving the Valley, regardless of where you are going next. It matches the last stop of one of the shuttles driving around the Valley and is called **Valley View**.

It is near the end of the one-way road section taking you out of the Valley. From there, you have a great view of El Capitan, the Merced River, Bridalveil Fall and, until a few years ago, a big dead tree inside the river.

Everybody wanted to be photographed there. Each time I was shooting from this spot tourists were asking me to take a picture of them standing on the tree.

ey View - The dead tree is no longer there. In 1997 this area was flooded

How could I deny as I had a camera hanging around my neck! The tree is gone. I still have the pictures. If you are not returning to June Lake but are staying in a location on the west side of the Park, you will more than likely exit using SR 41 to **Oakhurst** or SR 140 to **Mariposa**.

Both towns have nice places to stay and are a gateway to the Gold Country. Check Chapter 12 for more details on what to look for in the Gold Country. There is a lot of history there. Spending a few extra days along SR 49 is highly recommended if your schedule allows it.

Yosemite Valley

XIV

DEATH VALLEY NATIONAL PARK

Going to **Death Valley** and back to June Lake in one day is absolutely out of the question. However if you are in the Eastern Sierra and it is not in the hottest part of the summer, a trip to Death Valley should be orchestrated, if possible.

This should include at least one overnight stay. Many tourists find themselves simply driving through Death Valley, travelling from Las Vegas to Yosemite, without spending any quality time there.

In this chapter I describe my favorite spots in Death Valley so that if you go, you would not miss out on them.

Death Valley National Park, established on February 11, 1933, covers almost 3,000 square miles. It contains at the same time the lowest point in the western hemisphere, **Badwater,**

at -282 ft. below sea level, as well as the hottest spot in the world. This is, of course, in the summertime. Record temperatures of 135 degrees Fahrenheit have been recorded there. As the humidity in Death Valley is very low, the high temperatures can actually be very tolerable. However, it is still recommended to visit in the fall, winter or early spring.

There are two ways to drive from June Lake to Death Valley. In each case, it is about 200 miles one-way and one should assume that half of that distance is going to be 30-40 mph. But all the roads are excellent paved roads.

Just make sure you have a full tank of gas and enough water in your radiator. There are some spots along the way where water for the radiator is available..

The most common road to Death Valley is through Lone Pine. Take a right turn at the June Lake junction and drive for about 100 miles on US 395 until you reach Lone Pine, which we have visited in Chapter Ten. Turn left at the Visitor Center, not without looking inside first, of course, and check on the road conditions with the Park Ranger.. You are now on SR 190, only 100 miles from Death Valley, but you will have to cross three mountain ranges.

If you take the Lone Pine route your first stop should be the vista point at **Father Crowley Lookout**. You have a great view of the desert and the **Panamint Mountain Range**, the last range to cross.

The lookout was named after a Catholic Priest who ministered in the area in the 1930s. The highest peak in the

Opposite: Badwater. At -282 ft. this is the lowest spot in the western hemisphere.

Father Crowley Overlook - A fantastic view hard to capture on film

of your own footsteps, like I did. Late afternoon is the ideal time of the day to do so.

As a matter of fact, all activities in Death Valley should be done in the morning or in the afternoon. As a photographer, I appreciate the light conditions better; as a human being I appreciate the temperature better.

Around noon time there are only two places to consider in Death Valley: your airconditioned motel room or the very nice swimming pool at the Furnace Creek Ranch.

Panamint Range is **Telescope Peak**, over 11,000 ft. As the valley floor below is at -282 ft. this is possibly the biggest mountain-top-to-valley-floor view in the world.

Death Valley flower: desert five spot

Once you get closer to the valley you reach **Stovepipe Wells**. Note there are a lot of diabolic names in Death Valley. Stovepipe Wells has a restaurant and lodging facilities. I recommend you stay at the **Furnace Creek Ranch**, as it is closer to everything else.

Sand Dunes

However, a stop here is required as on the left hand side of the road you will see the famous **Sand Dunes** of Death Valley. Park your car, take a water bottle out of your cooler and go for a stroll over the dunes. Take a picture

Furnace Creek

It is not a long drive from Stovepipe Wells to Furnace Creek. I assume this is where you will spend the night. There is absolutely no point in driving through Death Valley during the hottest part of the day and continue on to, let's say, Las Vegas, without at least spending one night there.

Furnace Creek Ranch has nice motel rooms, a golf course even, a saloon, a steak house, a General Store and a small museum. Up the road is the Furnace Creek Inn, a very expensive hotel. Stay at the Ranch, have dinner, a couple of beers maybe, and go to bed early.

Zabriskie Point

My favorite photo moment was in Death Valley. I got up at 5 am and drove the 6 miles to **Zabriskie Point**, which you reach by continuing on SR 190. Do not take Badwater Road but drive past the Furnace Creek Inn, then turn right.

I set up my Hasselblad camera and waited for the sun to rise behind me. The temperature would also rise from 55 to 95 degrees in about one hour. But once the sun came up it lit the Panamint mountains across the valley first and then hit the top of the brown, sandy structure at Zabriskie point called **Manly Beacon.** I called

More Sand Dunes by Stovepipe Wells. Take a picture of your own footsteps!

ıd Dunes

this the golden moment. Gradually, the entire structure was covered with sunlight and I shot two rolls of film in 20 minutes.

Just two hours later I went to the Visitor Center and discovered greeting cards with a shot taken from the same spot, in color. On the back it said: *Copyright 1947, Ansel Adams.* This is one of his rare color photographs. I was there exactly 50 years later.

Zabriskie Point is named after Christian Brevoort Zabriskie of the Wyoming Territory, the vice-president and general manager of the Pacific Coast Borax Company in the early twentieth century. Borax was what people were mining for in Death Valley, so they could make soap from it. Zabriskie Point was also a 1970 movie by Michelangelo Antonioni.

Badwater

There are several other places that you want to visit if you are in Death Valley. The most obvious one is the already mentioned **Badwater**, about 20 miles from Furnace Creek.

Zabriskie Point during sunrise.

This is indeed the lowest spot in the entire western hemisphere: 282 ft. below sea level. There is a parking lot. Leave your car and walk towards Telescope Peak. You will see a small pond of salty water: Badwater. Now look behind you. Way above you on the hill in front of you is a white stripe and the words *Sea Level*.

In 1997, the same trip I took my first Zabriskie Point picture, I had a similar Ansel Adams moment when shooting at Badwater. Going there after the Zabriskie Point shoot it was obviously a little later in the morning but I still got some good shots.

Once I was done shooting and went to the Visitor Center I found that Ansel Adams greeting card of Zabriskie Point I mentioned, but also a Badwater one, similar to mine but with more pink. He must have gotten there earlier.

So the next morning I went back to Badwater for sunrise to catch some pink skies and guess what: a full moon!

In 2005 something unusual happened here. It rained! There was so much rain that a 3 mile lake developed near Badwater and people came there to do some Kajaking.

It was shown on CNN. That is why many people visited Death Valley that spring. Because of the rain there were also species of wildflowers nobody had seen in 30 years.

I went in April and caught the end of the lake and the flowers. The heavy rain had turned Zabriskie Point into a construction zone, as he road was washed away. Other places were not reachable as well. Everything should be restored to order now.

Artist Palette. Look at the different colors. A mistery of nature.

dwater with full moon at 5.30am

Artist Palette

Driving back from Badwater there are two more places to visit. First, there is **Artist Palette**. It is a one way road off Badwater Road, a little bit of a fun rollercoaster near the end. But the main attraction is Artist Palette itself whith nothing more than some sandy rocks, but they have all kinds of different colors: turquoise, pink, light blue, etc. Scientists are still struggling trying to explain this wonder of nature.

Golden Canyon

When you are almost back at Furnace Creek and if you planned for it, as you do not want to hike here in the middle of the day, stop at the **Golden Canyon** parking lot. From there you can do a hike through what is called the **Badlands** and walk all the way up to the back of Manley Beacon near Zabriskie Point. The views are spectacular.

View from Golden Canyon

10.000 beer bottles. At one point in time, around 1907, the town had a population of 10,000 people.

Dante's View

If you have the time, take the road to Zabriskie Point and keep going, then drive up to over 5000 ft. above the valley floor. ***Dante's View***, at 5,475 feet at the crest of the Black Mountains gives you a spectacular view of the entire valley more than 5,000 feet down below, Telescope Peak across from it, and the Sierra Crest behind it.

I had an interesting small adventure there. About one mile before the summit, a bunch of guys with Harley-

Rhyolite ghost stealing a bicycle ?

Rhyolite

There are many more interesting spots in Death Valley, described in the excellent guides available. I am only listing two more. If you take the road to Beatty, NV, which is also on US 95, stop 7 miles before it and check out ***Rhyolite***, a ghost town with statues of ghosts.

There is not much left of the buildings of the original town, mining what it was named after: rhyolite. One interesting place though, and managed by a living human non-ghost person, is the bottle house. It is made of about

Famous bottle house in Rhyolite

Davidsons started waving at me along the side of the road. I just kept going, for about 10 yards.

There was ice on the road and they were trying to warn me. I managed to turn around. So I was halted by ice at what is considered the hottest place on earth!

Check out the excellent Visitor Center near Furnace Creek Ranch and learn about all the other interesting placing you can visit in Death Valley, some of which would require a high clearance vehicle. Scotty's Castle is very popular but I have never made it inside. Nearby Ubehebe Crater is interesting as well.

Death Valley Junction

Just outside the Park, at the junction of SR 190 and SR 127, the road that comes from Baker and goes through Shoshone, an alternate road to Death Valley for Angelinos and a likely route for folks coming from Las Vegas is **Death Valley Junction**.

The main attraction there is the **Amargosa Opera House**. An Opera House in Death Valley ? Yes, and it is a one man, I beg you a pardon, one woman

Dante's View, 5000 ft. above the valley floor offers spectacular views

show. Marta Becket, who had appeared on Broadway in shows such as Showboat and A Wonderful Town was vacationing in Death Valley in 1967. She went to Death Valley Junction to have a flat tire repaired and, while waiting for her car, checked out the buildings.

She found a building that was actually a theater and really never left the place. The first years she started painting murals.

A year later, the first performance was given at the Amargosa Opera House. It is still part of a regular tourist tour. If your itinerary calls for going that way, stop at the Junction and at a minimum check the building.

Amargosa Opera House

Badlands near Zabriskie Point after sunset.

INDEX

SELECTED BIBLIOGRAPHY

I list here only those publications that have been of use in the making of this book. This bibliography is by no means a complete list of all the works and all the resources I have consulted in the course of the years, nor is it intended to be a complete reference on all the materials that are available on the Eastern Sierra.

Bean, Betty, *Horseshoe Canyon : a brief history of the June Lake Loop*, June Lake, Calif., June Lake Loop Women's Club

Bowker, Davin, *South Tufa: A self-guided walking tour* (Mono Lake Committee field guide series), Mono Lake Committee, Kutsavi Press,1998

Cain, Ella M., *The Story of Early Mono County*, San Francisco Fearon Publishers, 1961

Chalfant, W. A., *Story of Inyo*, Chalfant Press, June 1980

Clyde, Norman, *Close Ups of the High Sierra,* Spotted Dog Press, Bishop CA, 2004

Dedecker, Mary e.a., *Deepest Valley: A Guide to Owens Valley,* Its Roadsides and Mountain Trails, Mammoth Lakes, Calif., Genny Smith Books, August 1995

Farquhar, Francis P., *History of the Sierra Nevada* , Berkeley, University of California Press, June 1, 1965

Hill, Mary , *Geology of the Sierra Nevada* , Berkeley , University of California Press

Irwin, Sue, *California's Eastern Sierra: A Visitor's Guide*, Los Olivos, CA, Cachuma Press, 1991.

Johnson, Anne, *The Ancient Bristlecone Pine Forest*, Community Printing and Publishing, Bishop, CA, 1999

King, Clarence, *Mountaineering in the Sierra Nevada* (High Sierra Classics Series), Yosemite National Park, Calif., Yosemite Association, June 1997

Luce, Ron, *Easy Day Hikes Around Mammoth - Written and Illustrated by Ron Luce,* Ron Luce, Bishop, CA, 2003

Medley, Stephen, *The Complete Guidebook to Yosemite*, Yosemite National Park, Calif., Yosemite Association, August 2004

Olmsted, Gerald W., *Best Of The Sierra Nevada*, New York, Crown, 1991

O'Neill, John Carroll, *Tioga Tramps: Day Hikes in the Tioga Pass Region*, Albicaulis Press, June 2002

O'Neill, Elizabeth Stone, *Meadow in the Sky: A History of Yosemites Tuolumne Region,* Albicaulis Press, Groveland CA, May 1984
Olmsted, Gerald W., *Best Of The Sierra Nevada*, New York, Crown, 1991

Rinehart, Dean, Elden Vestal, and Bettie E. Willard, *Mammoth Lakes Sierra: A Handbook for Roadside and Trail* , Mammoth Lakes, Calif., Genny Smith Books. 7th Edition 2003

Rose,Gene, *Yosemite's Tioga Country a History and Appreciation*, Yosemite Association, Yosemite National Park, October 2006

Staff, University of Chicago Press (Editor), *The Chicago Manual of Style*, Chicago, University Of Chicago Press, August 2003

Storer, Tracy I., *Sierra Nevada Natural History* (California Natural History Guides), Berkeley, University of California Press, September 1, 2004

Tierney, Timothy, *Geology of the Mono basin* (Mono Lake Committee field guide series) , Mono Lake Committee, Kutsavi Press, 2000

Twain, Mark, *Roughing It* (Mark Twain Library), Berkeley, Univer sity of California Press.

Tweed, William C., *Death Valley and the Northern Mojave: A Visitor's Guide*, Los Olivos, Cachuma Press 2003